1

CUMBERLAND

ISLAND

A Place Apart

By

THORNTON W. MORRIS

The Cumberland Island Conservancy

CUMBERLAND ISLAND *A Place Apart*

Published by CIC Publishers • The Cumberland Island Conservancy, Inc.

1950 North Park Place, Suite 400, Atlanta, GA 30339

www.cumberlandisland.com

Copyright ©2008 Thornton W. Morris

Digital Offset Lithography by Boyd Printing, Panama City, FL, USA.

Text by Thornton W. Morris.

Book design and production by Digital Impact Design, Inc., Cornelia, GA

www.didmedia.com

Photography by Don Harbor and David Haynes, with additional photos by Barbara McDowell and Jim Boyd.

ISBN 978-1-60643-796-4

FIRST EDITION - July 2008

Foreword

The mission of The Cumberland Island Conservancy, Inc., is:

- TO SUPPORT educational and scientific research on Cumberland Island, Georgia.

- TO PROVIDE monetary and physical support for the preservation of Cumberland Island, and to work with the National Park Service as co-stewards in preserving this great natural, cultural, and historical resource.

- TO AID in the dissemination of educational and scientific information regarding Cumberland Island to the National Park Service, the public at large, and the residents of Cumberland Island.

This book by Thornton Morris, the President of the Conservancy, exists in order to tell, in a personal, and sometimes amusing, way, the story of how Cumberland Island was preserved and is now one of our nation's most treasured national seashores. It is a book about the relationship between life and death, a dynamic with which few of us consciously deal in the twenty-first century, but which is a day-to-day issue on Cumberland Island. It tells the story of why Cumberland was saved for future generations and the meaning of that preservation for all Americans.

Cumberland Island is a place that changes people. It has changed visitors and politicians, as well as the owners themselves. This book is a personal account of some of the emotional and spiritual values of those owners, and how they worked with a coalition of interested persons to keep Cumberland from being another housing development located on the Atlantic seaboard.

The challenge of the National Park Service is to find the balance between excessive use of Cumberland, which could actually damage the historical, cultural, and natural environment, and to provide access to the American public. And it is very important to remember that only by visiting Cumberland will people be changed by it. In order to effect the intent of those who worked so hard for its inclusion within the National Park Service, there must be access to it for the American public. Without access, the change which the owners desired, and the public fought for, will not take place.

The Conservancy supports a rational policy for the visitation of Cumberland Island, balancing its desire for Cumberland to touch people, while preserving its uniqueness. The Conservancy is disappointed with the continual conflicts generated by some environmental organizations, which are probably composed of well-meaning individuals, but which disseminate incorrect and politically motivated information. A part of the mission of The Conservancy is to act as a forum for truthful, rational, and non-politically motivated statements regarding Cumberland Island.

The Conservancy believes that Cumberland Island should be a place of peace. It should be a place of harmony. It should not be a place for partisan political conflict. The Conservancy desires to highlight Cumberland Island as a place of spiritual awareness, emotional growth, and intellectual stimulation. It hopes that this book will help in that endeavor.

THE BOARD OF DIRECTORS:

THE VERY REVEREND SAMUEL G. CANDLER
MR. FRANKLIN W. FOSTER
MR. PER G. H. LOFBERG
MR. THORNTON W. MORRIS
MR. GLENN D. WARREN

The Island that Transforms

Prior to publishing this book, I had two different editors look at it. Although the opinion of one was somewhat more direct (one might say harsher) than the other, both conveyed the same message: This manuscript has more "I's" and "me's" in it than you can shake a stick at. Both of them felt that with all of the "I's" and "me's" in it, the manuscript came across as more egocentric than they felt that I probably was in reality.

That, of course, then led me to the inevitable attempt to gain a broader audience and have the book less focused on me. After listening to the advice and pondering it

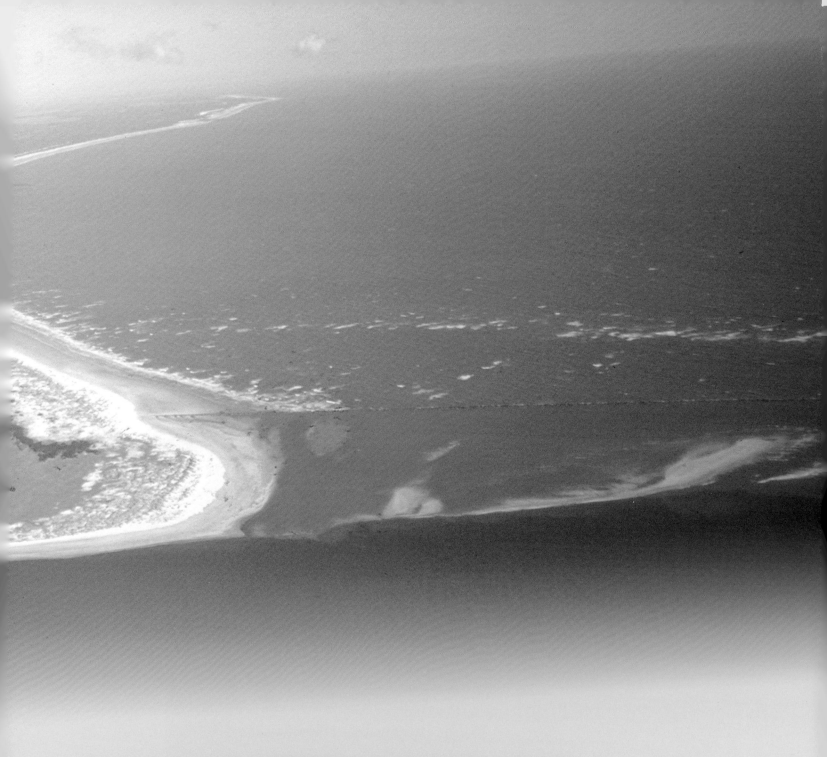

over a single malt one evening, I decided that even though they were probably right, it did not matter. This is a book which reveals me/my life on an island. I have used the first person more than in probably any writing I have ever done. (A part of that aspect causes me discomfort.)

These stories and vignettes are simply what happened to me. Sometimes I have told them with as straight a connection with my soul as possible. Other times I have simply passed along a humorous reflection. Other stories are more of an observation than anything else. I have attempted to be open, honest, and objective about what I experienced. I probably have some of the historical aspects off here and there, but this is not a historical journal. It is how an island and its inhabitants changed my life – in my opinion, for the better.

From the day when Bob Ferguson walked into my small office in a law firm in Brunswick, Georgia, my life was irrevocably changed. It was as though I jumped into a river and let it carry me wherever it was going. All I have to give to others is what I felt, what I saw, and what I did. I am using myself as a conduit to pass on to others the rewarding uniqueness of this experience. Please bear with me in that endeavor.

Also, please bear with me on inconsistencies and redundancies that might exist in the book. I wrote the stories at different times in history and during different periods of my life. Some were written when I was excited and high on life, others when I was just barely treading water to keep my head above the surface. Some of the writings are factual, others poetic, and some, like the one regarding tigers, just curious. And, each comes from a different place inside me.

For those people who don't like me anyway, this writing may well justify any claims of maniacal egotism. So be it.

As I think back upon the last 40+ years of my life on Cumberland Island, I realize that the natural areas on Cumberland have brought great serenity to me and have helped me, meditatively, to arrive at my present spiritual beliefs. Fully mature long-leaf pines tend to be more effective with me than spires and steeples. But the thing which has been the most effective in sculpting who I am today has been the people living on the Island. It was the people from whom I learned. They have tended to be the teachers of my life's lessons. And, although Cumberland is blessed with more natural, cultural, and historical resources than almost any place in the country,

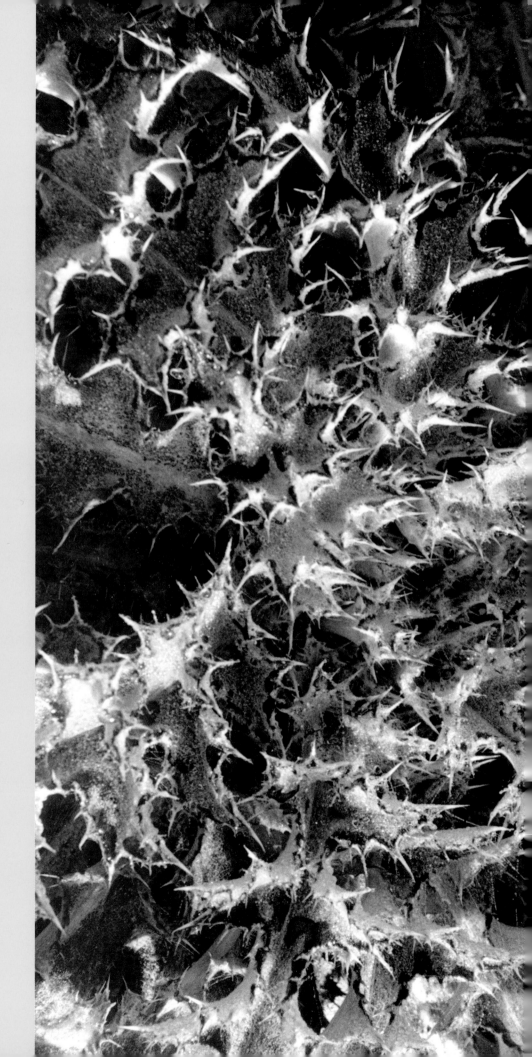

still it was the people, the living humans, who have affected me the most. And their stories are the essence of this book. Who else is there to explain the importance of Coley Perkins in the creation of the Cumberland Island National Seashore or to tell the funny stories about Lucy Ferguson? Or to share the lessons gained from trusting people like Onie Lee Butler? It is, after all, humans who leave the most pronounced impact on other humans. And we can only understand a natural area through the human perspective anyway.

This book was not prepared with any preconceived agenda, nor do I have any particular preference as to what you take from it. My only hope is that I am successful in imparting to the reader, through beautiful images of the natural, cultural, and historical wonders of the Island, how one individual born on a farm in northwest Georgia has been spiritually and emotionally imprinted by this most extraordinary jewel. ℒ❤

— Thornton W. Morris

Tides of Life and Death

Cumberland Island has been a retreat for me and my family for over thirty years — a very small drop in this barrier Island's historical bucket. We have all walked its trails and subtropical forests, fished and swum in its tidal creeks and shores, and ridden horses crashing through myrtle thickets and out onto the wide-open space of the endless beach beyond. We have eaten fresh oysters, herded cattle in the surf, slept, laughed, and dreamed — in short, we have done all the things one does to renew oneself so that the daily challenges of life can be faced gracefully when we must return to the man-made world of modern commerce.

This Island paradise has taught me many of the really important lessons in life. But more importantly, Cumberland Island has given to me a context within which I can face my own mortality. This was most profoundly shown to me when I witnessed, during a violent hurricane, the uprooting of a massive live oak whose breadth I could not even span. The elements' fury and destruction in bringing this enormous tree's death seemed brutal and final to me. Surely anyone who could witness such a fall would agree that death was rampant as the storm surged across the Island. And yet, one of the oak's acorns lodged in a crevice in the dead tree's truck. With the returning sun came a bud-like shoot of green. Stay for an afternoon or a week, and you will quickly see that life and death breathe the same breath of the tides on Cumberland.

But all this retreat is what we know as vacation. We have been blessed and privileged in our association with this special place because Cumberland Island truly is a wonderful and unique getaway. As I've gotten older and watched others playing in the same pristine creeks and sands as my children did before them, I realize this Island is not an escape at all but a place to come to ultimately. It is the vital part of who I have become on my earthly journey. My soul perches here for eternity like a great comical bird or one of the giant wood storks that lands awkwardly but resolutely in the pines at the edge of the inlet where we live.

Peace is when

time doesn't matter

as it passes by.

MARIA SCNELL

I see the birds and magnificent ospreys working their territory with some kind of crazy understanding of what eternity is, what being means, what death holds.

My first years on the Island were pure infatuation. Its beauty and mystery were obvious to me as they are to any visitor. But what I have come to experience in my later years is not so much the ecstatic playfulness of a new found love, but rather the evolved, mature and deeply profound love that comes from knowing a place (or a person) in all seasons and moods.

My life as an attorney in a large city has been satisfying and challenging in the ways I'd hoped for as a young man. But my other life – my life as a citizen of Cumberland Island – has been the singular force that shapes my soul. The solitude, the peace and quiet, the myriad of colors and shadows, the symphonies of sounds and smells – all of these are the elements of a life well lived that I want to pass on to my loved ones.

As I sit here in my old wicker chair on the point facing the sunset, I can sense the giant oaks wrapping their arms around my house at my back. I can see the millions of tiny animal footprints in the mud at my feet and can hear the murmur of the teeming world of the river beyond. From this enchanting vantage point, I know that, by attempting to share the Island with others, I really am a man with empty hands. There is nothing I can give them but the encouragement to open their eyes and hearts and, with a little nudge, head them into this eternal beauty.

The people who have inhabited this Island have also had a huge impact on me. The spirits of the ones who no longer leave footprints can be felt at any given moment of the day or night. I cannot explain this and have stopped trying to make sense of it, but every person is as unforgettable and unique as every storm. The Island forces all of their beautiful eccentricities to the surface, and we share our individual lives in ways that don't happen on the mainland. I am grateful for the wisdom and beauty imparted to me by every one of them, but especially Coleman Perkins, who provided me the land, and his cousin, Lucy Ferguson, who provided me the vision with which to see it.

This book is a collection of photographs and vignettes that I hope will serve as a message to your own soul. There is, quite simply, nowhere else on earth like Cumberland Island. It is this uniqueness that I hope you will feel as I have felt, and the idea that our purpose is somewhere entangled in all this beauty. ✍

The spirits of the ones

who no longer leave

footprints can be felt

at any given moment

of the day or night.

Stewards of This Land

I realized early on in my relationship with Cumberland Island that denying humans access to the Island is not a solution to saving it. In fact, I suggest that to do so is a naïve and sentimental indulgence in the belief that what is man-made is somehow not a part of the natural world; that things will be right with the Island only if human beings were left out of the picture. Life, and certainly not ecosystems, is not that simple.

I discovered Cumberland Island first in the papers and letters housed in the Georgia Room at the University of Georgia library when I was in law school in the mid-1960's. A fascination with history, especially colonial and ante-bellum Georgia, led me to the Noble Jones Collection where I spent hours pouring over the details of the everyday life of planters and other inhabitants of the region when I was supposed to be studying torts. There I discovered the workings of a sophisticated and intricate world of farming unique to the Southern coast.

The first ten years of my own life had been spent on a family farm in northwest Georgia, and while this farm was not the genteel, grand world of the coastal plantations, it was a connection to soil and gave me an early understanding of the labor and dedication to the land that was necessary for survival. Clearly though, it was my introduction to the concept of stewardship. This I could share with the

planters in my imagination, and perhaps this is what undergirded my relationship with Lucy Ferguson, who was a pivotal player in the Island's history.

My family did not vacation at the beach. I suppose that we could have afforded it, but taking leave of the necessary duties on a farm would have been incomprehensible to my grandfather, Seaborn Jones Whatley, who was responsible for our lives. Taking a break was quite a different matter. He even suggested that church duties at the Enon Baptist Church, where we attended, should never get in the way of going fishing and, according to my grandfather, the fish were always hungriest on Sunday morning. As my life was completely in the hands of my grandfather, my spiritual life was not to be nurtured in the established church but in the land and in the creeks.

A business proposition was what first brought me to Cumberland Island. Lucy Ferguson wanted to create a bona fide farming operation on the Island, which her wealthy New England family had been coming to for sport and recreation for over one hundred years. She was enough of a businesswoman to know that all the self-sufficiency in the world would not provide the hard cash necessary to pay taxes on the thousand-plus acres she owned. She had the idea that the house known as Greyfield could be turned into an inn and that her farm could be enjoyed by a limited number of paying guests who would bring income that was not detrimental to the Island.

In 1965, Robert W. Ferguson, Lucy's husband, came into the small law firm where I was working in Brunswick, Georgia, wanting to consult with someone on a tax return for a farmhand named Otis Harper. Bob was a handsome man with distinguished features representative of the patrician Yankee world from which he came. Unlike most of his fellow northern family members, he came south and became a Southerner. So did Lucy.

On the day I met Bob, he was just off a boat in the marsh and had come into town with his khakis rolled up to his knees exposing strong, lean legs caked in the slick gray mud of the marsh. From the waist up, he looked like any other genteel visitor — tweed jacket, pressed white shirt, and a straw hat. But that mud and those sock-less feet in old tennis shoes spoke of a gentleman of a different order — one who was on a mission, oblivious to what other people might think, living in the moment and under the influence of the natural world around him. I liked him immediately.

After dispensing with Otis's tax return, we turned to business and plans were made for me to visit the Island to meet Lucy and see the house and farm. The following weekend, I flew in a small plane over to Cumberland. It was a hot, dry day, and I waited somewhat dubiously for Bob to come pick me up in his truck. After awhile, I spotted a cloud of dust in the distance which proved to be a battered old Ford pick-up. He was at the wheel and in the back, standing and straddling the truck-bed, was what I took to be a farmhand; a small deeply-tanned woman who had the features of a Native American — a distinguished brow, intelligent, deep-set eyes, and a prominent nose. She leaned into the wind, her leathery hands gripping the roof of the truck while Bob spun across the pasture in the sand to where I was standing.

Without getting out of the truck, he motioned me inside to sit beside him as we headed back to Greyfield. His only acknowledgement of the woman onboard was to say in a rather friendly and casual but respectful voice, "We'll let the squaw ride in the back. She prefers it that way."

It wasn't until we'd been in the truck for several minutes that I realized that the unforgettable character hanging onto the back, still standing, still facing the direction we were traveling like a curious bird scouting a familiar hunting ground, was Lucy Carnegie Ricketson Ferguson. ❧

Natural Partners

Nature and her creative processes are vividly illustrated on long summer nights when loggerhead turtles emerge from the seas and make their way onto the shore to lay hundreds of eggs in the warm sand at the edge of the dunes.

Today, much is known about loggerheads and their annual migration from the ocean's depths to mainland seashores and barrier islands. Both Cumberland and Little Cumberland Island are now locations for a turtle protection and research program that was started by Ingram Richardson. Ingram was a resident of Little Cumberland Island when I first came to the Island.

Up until only about forty years ago, the fauna and flora of the Island were protected only by those living there. In those times, I used to wait for the turtles' emergence from the sea, watching the females arrive on the tide to begin their instinctual search for the perfect place to lay their eggs and bury them in the sand. Each loggerhead turtle seemed to know just where to find her perfect spot in the sand — just like salmon returning to the spawning stream or homing pigeons circling in the sky until they somehow sense the way to their coops below.

Watching this, I would stand motionless on the shore — a silent but respectful witness to a cycle of nature experienced by few mainlanders. Right in front of me, huge female loggerheads would emerge from the dark water and rise out of the waves like some strange amphibious, shell-encrusted sea craft. As they made their way toward the dunes, I could see that these magnificent creatures were maybe three feet across and even longer in length, and you could tell from their bulk that each turtle easily weighed over one hundred pounds. Their legs levitate their bodies like pontoons, and you can see from their labored but determined effort to get on shore that the place of their birth is no longer their preferred habitat.

When they are out of the water entirely and a safe distance on the shore, the females begin using their back flippers to dig large, deep holes perhaps one foot wide and a couple of feet deep. Then each female may deposit nearly one hundred eggs into what will soon be an underground nest, completely insulated and ready to bake her eggs, like adobe bricks, in the sun. The eggs, when first laid, look like ping-pong balls, but when they are completely deposited – a process that can take over an hour – the eggs glisten like stars in a constellation, heralds of a birth to come.

We all know that turtles, like dinosaurs, are ancient creatures. So this means that this egg-laying ritual is an event eons old. And this natural occurrence is probably a painful one, or at least I thought so as I watched the mother's eyes tear throughout this ordeal. Even the sheer effort of the process is dangerous. For whenever a female loggerhead lays her eggs, she is very vulnerable and can become easily disoriented just from sheer exhaustion. After covering their eggs completely with sand, the weary females occasionally struggle up the shore in the wrong direction and head directly for the sand dunes – not the ocean that is essential for the loggerheads' survival.

When this happened and we were watching, we would head the turtles in the right direction. But now we know that no one should ever even venture out on the beach when loggerhead turtles are laying their eggs. Today, thanks to the efforts of the natural sciences, we know that even a flashlight in the woods, or a light from a house, can cause a loggerhead's homing abilities to go awry. Now we understand just how fragile the ecology of Cumberland Island is and the need for these special turtles to be preserved, to thrive, and to continue living in this coastal paradise.

When dragging myself ashore once after my boat capsized with Scott, a friend, and me in it, and we were in the water for over an hour, I began to fathom how it must feel to be a female turtle coming ashore to lay eggs. Being unable to stand and crawling up on shore, only then to collapse, did I then begin to wonder how really hard it must be to perform this annual ritual. That experience on the river side of Cumberland Island helped me become a much stronger supporter of the preservation of loggerheads. ✍

Now we understand

just how fragile the ecology of

Cumberland Island is.

Lucy

For the 30-odd years until her death when I represented Lucy Ferguson as her lawyer, there were plenty of serious matters to work on. But when Lucy was around, she always had the ability to laugh about the serious. She could bring humor into almost every situation.

Lucy was a Massachusetts girl who became a hard-and-fast Southerner. And so did her husband, Robert W. Ferguson. Bob, who came from Maine, so adapted to the Georgia environment that he was the first, so I am told, Yankee to be elected to the Georgia legislature since Reconstruction.

Lucy always viewed Cumberland as a place apart. Although it is a part of Camden County, Georgia, she always referred to the mainland as the "Main" or "over in the county." It was Lucy who cemented the relationships between the residents of the mainland and those of the Island. To everyone on the mainland, whether bankers, farmers, politicians, or whomever, she was always referred to as "Miss Lucy." She loved the plainness of the local character, and the people of Camden County loved her. And she never went lacking for help from the local citizens over on the mainland. Toward the end of her life, Camden County established a Lucy Ferguson day. I cannot remember what day of the year it is.

From the first day I met Lucy, gazing over the cab of that pick-up truck, her nose forward like the beak of an eagle, I knew that she was the most unforgettable character I had ever met. She still is, 16 years after her death.

I was told that Lucy was deaf from the age of six. I suppose that this handicap helped drive her to a life on a natural island, rather than one in Greenwich, Boston, Manhattan, or possibly Pittsburgh. She was never able to hear in a crowd, and she

disliked drinking alcohol. Cocktail parties were not her thing. She told me once that when in a crowd, all she could hear was a dull roar. She could not understand any particular person and the distraction kept her from reading lips, which got her into a lot of interesting situations.

One such time was when Secretary of the Interior Stewart Udall came to Cumberland Island to express interest on behalf of the National Park Service to the family's desire to preserve this Carnegie treasure. As the helicopters came in, Lucy became disoriented with the thump, thump, thump of its engines and began to chatter with someone about who knows what. Whatever it was, knowing Lucy, it was more interesting to her than meeting some Washington politician.

Since Lucy's support was always felt to be essential by the National Park Service to gain legislation for a national park at Cumberland Island, Mr. Udall wanted to meet Lucy as soon as possible. As one of the family members was shepherding Mr. Udall up to meet Lucy, she was busy in her new discussion. Not being able to hear the person introducing her to Mr. Udall, Lucy greeted the unknown visitor with her hand outstretched, offering a warm handshake greeting. Then, with the thump, thump, thump dying down, Lucy explained, "I know you..." The look on Mr. Udall's face was that of a politician being recognized, or as some of the people in Camden County might say, the smile on the face of a hog in slops. But it did not last long. What she explained was, "I know you....you are the shoemaker at Fernandina Beach." As the smile receded from Mr. Udall's face to an expression of perplexed insecurity, the amused relative immediately began to explain to Lucy that she had made a mistake and this was the United States Secretary of Interior. Finally Lucy, remembering why she was in the yard at Plum Orchard to begin with, realized that she had just called the Secretary of Interior a shoemaker from Fernandina and, in her own delightful way, simply said, "I am always getting people confused....and how is Washington these days? Is the President well?" While the others were shocked over the faux pas (which Lucy always called fox paws), Lucy was generally unperturbed and probably did not give a flip what Mr. Udall thought. Thus began the continuing saga of Lucy Ferguson vs. the National Park Service.

Of course Lucy actually supported the National Park Service coming to Cumberland, but you would never have known it by talking with her. Her take was that over half of the people who worked for the National Park Service were idiots, and she had not made up her mind about the other half. It did not help the day that one of the new (of many) superintendents followed the ritual of making a call, early in his tenure, on "Miss Lucy." This particular superintendent knew very little about the world of nature, and nothing about Cumberland. His wife, in an effort to be helpful, explained to Lucy that she loved wildlife. And then she asked, "Is that a stuffed bald eagle on your wall?" Lucy, who often had a very sharp tongue when she did not approve of someone, in a rare projection of graciousness simply replied, "No, that is not a bald eagle; it is a dead pelican which we found on the beach." After the new and uninitiated superintendent left, Lucy turned to me and, in no uncertain terms, told me never to bring some "damn fool" like that by to see her again. It seemed like she was angry with me for over a week for being a supporter of the National Park Service.

When the National Park Service Bill was working its way through Congressional committees during 1971 and 1972, the Senators from Georgia, of course, contacted Lucy to see if it was a thumbs-up or thumbs-down for the National Park Service. When we were in the Senate hearing, Senator Herman Talmadge wanted to make sure he knew how Lucy stood on the legislation. Lucy was flanked on her right by her son-in-law, Putnam McDowell, and by me on her left. It was here that the National Park

Service director, George Hartzog, committed to respecting Lucy's rights to private ownership of her land on Cumberland and thanked the entire Carnegie and Candler families for protecting Cumberland for the previous one hundred years. Since the only consistent thing in Lucy's life was her own inconsistency, neither Putty nor I knew what to expect from Lucy as she testified before Congress. When the question was finally put to Lucy as to whether she supported or opposed the Park Service's introduction to Cumberland Island, she turned to each of us and asked, in her typical adopted south Georgia manner, "Okay, boys, what do you think?" Putty and I assured her that we believed that the Park Service would respect her rights, and she gave Senator Talmadge the nod that she supported the legislation. That assurance was what was needed in order to get the Bill passed. And the Park Service has, in fact, respected its commitment to the Ferguson family, as well as its commitments to the other owners of Cumberland Island.

Most of the people who remember Lucy have recollections of her doing funny things. She lived in a world of humor. On one such occasion, she came to my home one afternoon mad as a wet hen, demanding that I come out to the beach to take some imprints of a jeep tire track. It appeared that Lucy had been sunbathing on the beach (age 85 years old), was "off the air" (she had turned her hearing aid off) and had fallen asleep in a natural condition (in the vernacular of most Georgians, "butt naked"), when someone driving down the beach saw her. While circling her several times (referred to on Cumberland as "doing donuts") they must have had quite an amusing few minutes. Apparently tiring of it, they continued down the beach. After calming her down, her farm manager/driver/good friend J. B. Peeples and I convinced her that possibly the best course of action would be to do nothing. Why cause a ruckus about the matter when probably no one would believe the person anyway? Somehow she had gotten in her mind that it was a shortcoming of the National Park Service, in its patrolling of the Island, which allowed the incident to occur. Neither J. B. nor I, as we both were choking back laughter, ever even mentioned to Lucy that possibly her own actions might have had a wee bit to do with the situation.

The Lucy Ferguson stories can go on and on for hours. Cumberland Island, this place apart, has produced some unusual characters. ✐

Lucy always viewed Cumberland as a place apart.

Resurrection

Lessons come from everywhere I am told.

I ask for some direction but there are just too many trees.

Too much confusion. No clear message.

The Island is easier for me to understand and

I search for answers here.

On the trail to the beach a magnificent oak has died and fallen.

On the inside, decay and emptiness.

Meditating on the message of "life after death" gives me some relief.

The ocean's waves in the distance invigorate me.

I think about the first life that washed ashore

or crawled out of this primeval marsh.

The pain in my stomach reminds me that I am frightened of the recent

changes in my life.

The fallen oak is an answer I do not want.

Three months pass, a change of seasons.

I return home from the beach one day to see

the same dead limbs and trunk on the floor of the forest.

Then, looking closer, I see the new beginning green:

five inches of life emerging from the center of the stump.

The Island is raw, unforgiving, but wise and complete too.

I see its cycles

and

I am beginning to understand my own life. ✐

Coley: Captain of Change

Coleman C. Perkins was a family leader during the period of the division of Cumberland Island into individual ownership after the death of Florence Nightingale Carnegie Perkins, his mother, thus dissolving the trust of Lucy Coleman Carnegie. Coley, along with Joseph C. Graves, a member of the Johnston branch of the Carnegie family and a resident of Lexington, Kentucky, and Putnam B. McDowell, then a son-in-law of Lucy R. Ferguson, were the officers of the Cumberland Island Company and helped guide the family through what could have been a very contentious period. The Carnegie family accomplished, with a minimal amount of ruffled feathers, that which many families fight through at least one or two generations. The division of the family's "jewel of the crown" among the heirs resulted with most every family branch seeing the division as a win for all. Coley was, I believe, viewed at the time as an "elder statesman" and a family member with the ear of all five branches.

After the division, where each of the five branches of the Carnegie family received a northern tract and a southern tract, Coley and his sister, Margaret P. Laughlin decided to divide their two tracts with Coley taking the northern tract (tract N-4) and Peggy taking the southern tract (tract S-1).

Coley built a dock at Squawtown and, thereafter, small cabins referred to as the "bunk house" and "pump house." At first the idea was for his family to have a place to dock their sailboat, which at the time was a gorgeous 45-foot Dutch Boyer Boat named Schollevaer. She had classic stained glass windows, an antique diesel engine, and a coke oven for heating the galley. Coley and his wife Posy, the former Elizabeth Boyd of Pittsburgh, Pennsylvania, sailed her to Cumberland at least a couple of times for the winter. She was laden with finished teakwood, and both Coley and Posy wanted her north as soon as the southern sun began to blister the varnish. This beautiful sailboat was my introduction to sailing. It was like a pilot beginning his career on the Concorde.

Coley's grandparents,
Thomas and Lucy Carnegie, built Dungeness.

I sailed with Coley and Posy in the south, around the Cumberland area, and north through the waters of Long Island Sound. Once when they were in South Dartmouth, Massachusetts, at the New Bedford Yacht Club, Thornton Jr. and I went out for a week-long cruise through the Elizabeth Islands, visiting Martha's Vineyard, Nantucket, and many of the small areas off Cape Cod. It seemed that with the sale of the Schollevaer, the end of the Golden Era, as Coley called it, came crashing down around the Carnegie family. Although some branches did better than others, on the whole, the large body of the accumulated wealth had lasted about four generations. I worked with the members of the family who had to transition from the period where there was enough inherited wealth so that a person did not have to maintain a job or profession, to where living off of the inheritance would not provide enough to support the cost to carry the inherited assets such as Cumberland Island. That transition has given to me an additional appreciation of the challenges to the individuals who inherit the wealth of their parents and grandparents. The boat was sold after Coley died in January, 1975.

The chance that Coley Perkins and I would develop a relationship as best friends was slim. Coley was probably thirty years older than me, and our lifestyles, at least on the surface, were different. I was an attorney who worked in an office every day and grew up with no money; Coley was a gentleman farmer and sailor from a famous family. Instead of listening to an occasional Episcopal liturgy, I was forced to absorb the ranting of some fire and brimstone Baptist preacher. It was the things that were similar about us that brought us together. We both owned and lived on a farm. We both loved and respected the wildness of Cumberland Island. We both related to the uneducated and "simple" country people of Camden County, and we both enjoyed staying at the Plaza Hotel in New York City. As a matter of fact, for several years during Coley's youth, his mother had an apartment at the Plaza, so I am told, and he spent many hours playing in Central Park. We both enjoyed boilermakers, a liter of beer with a shot glass filled with one's favorite whiskey dropped into the middle of it. That was back in my twenties, when I enjoyed drinking alcohol and did not wake up the next morning worshipping the porcelain god. Once Coley and I spent a week together at his farm in Connecticut touring all of the bars and saloons on the Connecticut River from Long Island Sound northward up river. My favorite was the Griswold Inn.

Lucy Ferguson once told me a story about Coley, and when I asked him about it, he just laughed. I took that to mean that there was some truth to it. It seems that Bob Ferguson was in the Georgia legislature, being the first Yankee to be freely elected to the Georgia

I worked with the members of the family who had to transition from the period where there was enough inherited wealth so that a person did not have to maintain a job or profession, to where living off of the inheritance would not provide enough to support the cost to carry the inherited assets such as Cumberland Island.

*The Carnegie stewardship has been one of holding the Island for
approximately one hundred years in its natural state, and then
lateralling the bulk of it to the National Park Service in a condition
that allowed the Island to immediately become one of the most
treasured National Seashores within the Department of the Interior.*

legislature since the 11 year martial law imposed by Reconstruction on the Confederate States. Lucy was with Bob in Atlanta staying at an old political haunt at the time, the Henry Grady Hotel. It seems that there was a winding staircase in the lobby of the Henry Grady Hotel extending up to the second floor. Coley was in basic training at Fort Benning, GA, located near Columbus, GA, and was the proud owner of a Harley-Davidson motorcycle. The story goes that he drove the Harley-Davidson to Atlanta to visit his cousin, Lucy, and her husband, Bob. By the time he got to Atlanta, Coley was lucky to be able to keep the bike upright. Those were the days when drinking while driving was seen more as a fun time than as a murderous activity as we now view it. And probably being drunk on a motorcycle might be suicidal rather than murderous anyway.

After going up and down Peachtree Street and finally locating the Henry Grady Hotel, Coley apparently decided to bypass the formality of checking with the concierge and proceeded to drive his motorcycle into the lobby of the Henry Grady up the stairs to the second floor and only stopped when he stalled out about four steps from the top. The bike then began to tumble backwards, Coley jumped off, and it crashed into the lobby. It seems no one was hurt, and since Bob Ferguson was a legislator, after a few dollars passing hands, everyone was happy. I never found out whether he was able to drive the bike back to Columbus, GA, or if he ended up catching a bus like most of the service people did during World War II.

As I said, Coley and I developed a very close relationship. I think he was able to form close relationships, maybe better than I was at the time. However it happened, it made me feel comfortable and I was open to his friendship.

Coley died during the early part of 1975. Even during the joy and beauty of my marriage ceremony with Annette in February of that year, I still missed Coley not being there and offered a prayer of remembrance for him.

I was impressed with Coley and Posy's relationship. Posy was a Pittsburgh socialite and fox hunter, who married Coley for a rural and Island lifestyle. I don't know if she missed the gaiety and parties of a Pittsburgh lady, but in my conversations with her over the years, she simply referred to that as a previous part of her life and that her life now was with Coley, their farm, the Island, and their boat. Fox hunting and its like were to be things of the past for her.

Coley and Posy seemed to depend on one another. I never remember seeing one without the other. It always seemed to me to be a partnership between the two, and it appeared appealing.

The idea that Coley might want to "get away" from Posy, or Posy from Coley, just seemed, even now, to be foreign from what either of them would think. I only heard Posy praise Coley and give him support. And when speaking of Posy, Coley did so with the utmost respect and admiration. I hope one day to be in a place where I can experience personally what I observed in them.

Their children seem to have been able to select partners with whom they have held together marriage relationships. I suspect that it has something to do with what they picked up as children and young adults while living with Coley and Posy.

One of the largest assets of the Carnegie family was Cumberland Island, Georgia. With its eighteen-plus miles of beaches, its thousands of acres of pristine virgin forest, and its miles and miles of marsh-front property, the Carnegie family was presented with a dilemma.

There was no dilemma at all for Lucy Ferguson. "Our family will hold the property for another hundred years!" But for individuals like her astute son-in-law, Putty McDowell, and family members like Coley Perkins and Joe Graves, the family had to find an answer to the "question of Cumberland."

The Old Hotel at High Point, now a personal residence of the Candler family of Atlanta

Most all of the members of the Carnegie family saw Cumberland as a single unit. Even after it had been divided between the various family members, it was still seen as a whole – a family heritage. And the family wanted to be good stewards of this heritage. They did not want it to be another Jekyll Island, which they had seen in the previous twenty years go from an island like Cumberland to a haphazard development experiment by the State of Georgia. Nor did they want it to be an extension of the Florida growth. The Carnegie stewardship has been one of holding the Island for approximately one hundred years in its natural state, and then lateralling the bulk of it to the National Park Service in a condition that allowed the Island to immediately become one of the most treasured National Seashores within the Department of the Interior. The idea that Cumberland Island might become developed was repugnant to the Carnegie family.

The core question which had to be answered by the leaders of the family was that of how to hold a non-income producing asset over the long haul, where that asset has a continually increasing tax basis. Family members like Coley, Joe, and Putty saw all too clearly the future of accelerating tax liability and the corresponding pressures for sale and development in order to meet that liability. It became apparent that for the next hundred years and on, Cumberland needed to be held by a tax-exempt entity, preferably one which was well funded. After checking off many of the major conservation organizations due to the depth (or rather non-depth) of their pockets, consistently the solution was the National Park Service. After all, it had kept a focused eye on Cumberland since shortly after the Second World War to see if it might become available as a national park.

The ultimate turning point came when two tracts of land on Cumberland sold to Charles Fraser, the developer of Hilton Head Island, South Carolina. Charles was never able to acquire any more property on Cumberland, although he made an all-out effort to buy all of it. Because of political complications, he was never able to develop his own tract, but he did cause the hard decision to be reached on the "Cumberland question" by the Carnegie family. The Carnegies teamed up with the owners of the northern portion of Cumberland, the conservation-minded Candler family from Atlanta, and invited the National Park Service to come to Cumberland to begin acquiring parcels of real estate as they became available. Unlike many national parks where there exists an adversarial relationship between the residents and the National Park Service, that has not been the case at Cumberland.

The National Park Service was originally introduced to Cumberland Island by members of the Carnegie family, the Johnston branch who called Lexington, Kentucky, home, and the residents and the National Park Service have maintained a tradition of "co-stewardship" during the period while private ownership exists. Cumberland is an example of where private equity can work hand in hand with public ownership, when both groups take a reasonable and considered approach to the issues affecting the area. (For the approximate 35 year period that the Cumberland Island National Seashore has been in existence, the National Park Service and the Cumberland residents have worked together effectively as co-stewards for this great national heritage. The greatest challenges have come from individual special-interest pressure groups, primarily environmental organizations, which have agenda of their own which go far beyond the boundaries of Cumberland.)

In 1970, the National Park Foundation acquired the holdings of Charles Fraser, the Johnston family, and Coley Perkins. These three tracts of land were sufficient to meet the requirements of the Andrew Mellon Foundation, which triggered its commitment to contribute money to make the Cumberland Island National Seashore a reality.

Coley Perkins did not want to sell his property to the National Park Foundation. He preferred to keep it for later generations. The reason he sold was to meet the requirements of the Andrew Mellon Foundation. Had he not sold, there would probably be no Cumberland Island National Seashore today. If there is one unsung hero whose actions directly contributed to the preservation of Cumberland as a member of the National Park community, it was Coleman Carnegie Perkins.

And he made available to me a small tract of land upon which to build my home on Cumberland Island. ✑

AUTHOR'S NOTE: *It was when he decided to transfer his land to the National Park Service that Coley asked me whether I would like to take the opportunity to obtain a home-site on Cumberland. I jumped at the idea and he showed me the tract he had in mind. At the time, and even today, I would have been happy if it had been at the bottom of a pit. The fact is that MorrisTown is in one of the most beautiful settings I have ever viewed. MorrisTown is located immediately north of Squawtown, the area Coley retained for himself and his family, and it borders a small tidal creek which divides the Squawtown property from that of MorrisTown. It is approximately 15 acres and is bounded on the west by the marsh, the south by the tidal creek, the east by the Main Road, and the north by the division line of Tract N-4 (the Perkins tract) from that of Tract N-5 (the tract which had been acquired by Charles Frazer). As I sit on my porch today, I can look north and see the area where, had Coleman Perkins not heeded the call of stewardship, I would be looking at condominiums and townhouses. As it is, I look at pristine forest, wild horses, the occasional deer, scavenging raccoons, and the rooting armadillo. Very few natural treasures have been saved in quite the way Cumberland was.*

Cumberland is an example of where private equity can work hand-in-hand with public ownership.

Serendipity

fter coming home from fishing at the jetties late one afternoon, I decided to stop by Greyfield for a beer. The jetties, which are located at the southern tip of Cumberland, are a string of huge boulders extending a couple of miles or so out to sea. They are a good place to catch fresh mullet, and I had a bucket full.

Greyfield is the large family Victorian house located on the main road near the southern end of Cumberland. It was converted from Lucy Ferguson's dwelling into an Inn around 1966. Greyfield was Lucy's childhood home.

As I came in the back door, I met Mitty Ferguson who was talking with the mainland on the VHF radio in the old kitchen. He had just returned to the Island on the Robert W. Ferguson, the large pontoon-type boat maintained by Greyfield, from Fernandina Beach, Florida. He suggested that I take a look into the back seat of the old, beat-up station wagon parked behind the house. For some reason, Lucy Ferguson owned some of the worst junk vehicles I have ever seen. This one was no exception.

Checking out what was in the vehicle was not an unusual suggestion.

After signing the "Honest-John" chit at the bar for the beer, I began walking toward the ancient automobile. It was early dark and my mind was racing through things I had seen in the back of cars on Cumberland: giant sea turtle shells, a dead turkey, a huge fish caught that morning, you name it. When I approached the vehicle, the sky was red with the setting of the sun over the marsh and the lights from Greyfield only flickered on the old car. As I was focusing my eyes as they were pressing against the half-raised back window, attempting to look inside, one of the beasts opened its huge jaws and let out a roar that was deafening. I fell back away from the car and had to pick my heart up off the ground. No animal on Cumberland had ever delivered such a blast before. And those teeth! Several inches long and gaping out of the black abyss of the giant cat's maw. I had just met two full-grown Indian tigers — a Bengal and a Black. Humans are not prepared for the roar of a tiger six inches away. I staggered back into Greyfield, and my pulse slowing, returned to its usual pace.

As was often the case with Lucy Ferguson, animals were as welcome to her aerie as any humans, perhaps more so. The tigers spent the night at her house, Serendipity, where she moved after Greyfield became the Inn. They slept in the bedroom of J.B. Peeples, her farm manager, who was on the mainland for the night. J.B. stomped around the house for weeks when he found out that two tigers had slept in his bed. The tigers' owners, members of the Ringling Circus, had been on their way to Sarasota when Lucy and Mitty spied them in traffic in Fernandina Beach while running errands. The story has it that Mitty and Lucy, fascinated and intrigued, chased them down, pulled them over like traffic cops, and one thing led to another. They all spent the night on Cumberland.

The two tigers were exercised on the beach the following morning at low tide. As the shore birds dodged the incoming waves as they broke on the hard sand, I wonder if they paused to gaze at the shoulder and hip muscles of the tigers as their paws dug into the sand. Or if the Osprey mother fishing for her hatchlings looked at the gleaming shiny coats against the grayness of the sandy beach. I would have enjoyed watching the local graduate student naturalist scratching his head as he inspected the tracks in an attempt to figure out what had just run down the beach.

I have always been curious as to whether the royalty of India were ever successful at hunting other game with these most perfectly sculptured beings.

It is hard for me to think about our losing the large cats. As the world goes industrial and with the multiplying population that requires to be fed, the eternal conflict of humans versus the wild tends to be lost for the beings that do not carry guns. I have heard various estimates as to when most of the large cats will be extinct, and it does not sound very encouraging. I suppose that we will have house cats around for quite awhile, but the idea that the tigers, lions, panthers and other large cats are in a decline seems sad, especially after being close to these physically perfect creatures. Their muscle texture, the sheer size and body weight, are all extremes I had never thought of until seeing those tigers on Cumberland. Except for a few isolated parks in India, Africa, and other parts of Asia and South America, it just doesn't seem that they will have much of a chance. Maybe our grandchildren and then theirs may be able to see them in zoos, but it just doesn't seem likely that the large cats will be able to make it much past the 21st century.

J.B. stomped around the house for weeks when he found out that two tigers had slept in his bed.

Reflections on Gene Poole

he area on Cumberland where I built my home was christened "MorrisTown" by Coleman Carnegie Perkins, and the name stuck. Coley, as he was known by most of the residents of Cumberland, was the grandson of Thomas M. and Lucy C. Carnegie. He was a first cousin and good friend of Lucy R. Ferguson. Coley was one of those people who combined a very quick mind with a dry sense of humor.

Although I received my real estate in 1970, I did not begin to build my house until 1974. It was a country type house, with a front porch for gazing over the marsh while rocking in the large chairs, and the back with a screened porch and large eating area. From 1974 through 2000, MorrisTown had only one makeover in 1991. We did some minor work on the structure and repainted the whole house. My main request was to be able to reach the kitchen and bathroom cabinets.

And the reason that I could not reach the kitchen and bathroom cabinets was that the original house was built by Gene Poole.

I was having a barn repaired at Harlech Farm, my farm in northwest Georgia, during 1973. I described this area on Cumberland to the workers during a lunch break one day and said that I wanted to get a small house built on it. With that, Gene Poole spoke up and said that he would build the house. It had never occurred to me prior to that point that Gene would know how to build a house. He was working for another farmer/local contractor as a day laborer. He then proceeded to talk me into seeing a house that he had just finished near Harlech Farm, and we visited the house later that afternoon. It looked acceptable and we agreed to a timetable for construction.

Gene was 6' 7" tall, as I recall, and probably weighed about 190 pounds. He was tall. And everything he built was tall. He placed the kitchen cabinets so high that he had to build a stool for me to be able to retrieve a glass or a plate for lunch. The bottom of the basins of the lavatories in the bathroom never got properly cleaned because I was never able to see them over the side of the cabinets. The first question that guests always asked was why everything was so high. I never really came up with a story that was shorter than 30 minutes that made any sense, and I think I finally just started saying that the builder liked it that way.

I was never able to blame Gene for long because the hiring of employees for a wilderness Island becomes an impossible situation. On the first trip down, we loaded a two ton truck from Harlech Farm, the Big Truck, with large rock from Berry College for the fireplace, piled on saws, hammers, cement mixers, plywood for forming and anything else we could think of. Gene drove Big Truck. I followed in my new Volvo sedan. I had just gotten it and still had the typical male fanaticism of not having one speck of dust on it. It was immaterial that within a year I knew that it would look like a junk pile anyway. However, it was still in the no-speck period of life.

Early on that summer Saturday morning, I drove to Gene's house to meet him and then pick up the three workers whom he had employed. Thornton Jr. and a covey of his friends had loaded up the trailer with probably four or five small motorbikes. When we picked up the first workers from their homes, I thought that the morning would be rather uneventful. I had mistaken the selection of Gene's companions. When we went into a small village outside Rome, Georgia, still early Saturday morning, me trailering motorbikes and following Gene in Big Truck, he mentioned casually that I might want to park about a block away from the house, the front of my car in the direction of the highway. Gene finally got the truck turned around in a too-small driveway, half knocking down some poor fellow's mailbox. I suggested that we fix the mailbox before picking up the person whom Gene said was named Gerald, but they all called Geraldine. I never understood the significance of the name. At any rate, Gene thought it best to pick up Geraldine and then we fix the mailbox and leave.

We all proceeded to the house in which Geraldine lived with his new wife of about thirty days. It would probably be off the mark for me to refer to them as still being on honeymoon.

Geraldine weighed in at about 135 pounds; the wife at about 250. And she did not come across to me as a kind and loving 250 pounds of marshmallows either. When Gene finally got Geraldine to the door, after knocking and hollering so loudly that any curious neighbor would be watching, Geraldine could not communicate to Gene quickly enough not to mention that they were going away for several months. Gene blurted out, "whar's yore bags, boy, we gotta go to Florida." With that, even though I was just outside the front porch, I both heard and felt the oncoming rage of a woman who had just been told that her husband of about 30 days might be leaving for a few months to go to Florida. The first discernable words I heard, at about the same time as the thud, were something like "you G... D... Sum-Bitch," and I saw Geraldine crumble after being hit by what appeared to be a ball bat across the side. I never understood why one of the guys knew that Geraldine had hidden his packed bag under the bed, but he did, and he ran into the bedroom. "Mrs. Geraldine" caught Geraldine heading to the bedroom at the door and pushed him onto the bed, mounting him with her knees over his arms, and began slugging him back and forth with her right and left fists. As one of the workers pulled the bag from under the bed, getting it caught by the springs which were bouncing up and down and ripping the front off, the other guy laid a flying body block on what was Floyd County's answer to the female sumo wrestling profession, knocking her off Geraldine and onto the floor.

After witnessing this in sheer disbelief, I began to run to the Volvo with a profound desire to get the hell out of there. So did all of the other males in the group. I looked behind me and saw Gene running ahead of the boys, followed by Geraldine who was somewhat crippled by the blow of the bat, with his face bleeding, and an arm over one of the others, all running toward the truck. It did not give me any security at all when I heard Gene hollering to Geraldine, asking whether there was a gun in the house and if she knew how to use it. I now understood why we parked down the street. My son and his friends, as they waited in the car ready to go, thought they were reliving some episode out of the Keystone Cops. The green Volvo, with its smell of new leather and loaded with the trailer of motorbikes, made the first corner, as best I recall, on two wheels never coming out of low gear. Big Truck kept all tires on the road, but I had never seen it go so fast. Gene had gotten into the driver's seat and had the motor revving when the fallen comrade was pushed in on the shotgun side with another diving in behind. The rear was brought up by the largest of the group who could only grab the window-facing, stand on the running board, and hold on for dear life.

I had no desire to stop, assuming that if she had a shotgun, she knew how to use it and probably also had access to a car. But I was feeling somewhat guilty and, after a couple of blocks, thought we should stop for a second when I saw the waist, and then the knees, and finally the shoes of the one on the running board go through the window, with arms pulling him along. From my rear-view mirror, I could not distinguish between head and feet, but I assumed that all four were in the cab of Big Truck, and both Gene and I floored it for the next thirty or so miles until we felt that the coast was clear. We then pulled over at a truck stop, gassed-up, had coffee and donuts, and I met the people who had been selected by Gene to build my dream home.

Unfortunately, the excitement of that particular trip did not end when we hit Highway 411 South and were outside of gunshot range.

The plan was to have me lead the way and Gene would follow by eyesight. Gene could not read a map. And somehow it never dawned on anyone to give any of the three others a map or, for that matter, anything else. From Highway 411 we took Interstate 75 and headed south. We started making good time after we got through Atlanta, and I was impressed on how the Big Truck was performing. Gene, I later understood, never took the accelerator off of the floorboard. They would fly by me going downhill and I would then pass them going back up the next. I mistakenly thought that it was all a game. That's just the way that Gene operated throughout his whole life. Right before we turned to proceed east on Highway 82 at Tifton, Georgia, Gene passed me and I thought it would be okay for him to lead the way for a while. In retrospect, I cannot image what good I thought was going to come from that decision.

As I was driving through Tifton, I noticed that Gene was going way too fast. In an attempt to catch up with him, I went over what is now referred to in our family as the famous Tifton railroad tracks at too high a rate of speed, coupled with all of the weight in the trunk of the car and the bike trailer, and somehow the frame of the car got caught on the railroad tracks. And the car stopped. Very quickly. It stopped so quickly that it crunched the frame, the area between the front and back doors began to look like an accordion, or maybe a folded piece of paper. At any rate, the car was ruined. And I could see Gene not looking back as he sailed out of Tifton. He was heading east.

"Mrs. Geraldine" caught Geraldine heading to the bedroom at the door and pushed him onto the bed, mounting him with her knees over his arms, and began slugging him back and forth with her right and left fists.

As we were causing the first traffic jam in Tifton, Georgia, in the last 30 years, I got out of the car, sat down on the railroad track and stared at my new, but now destroyed Volvo. I did all in my power to bring up some emotion. But nothing. All I could do was look at it in total astonishment. After realizing that I was not going to be able to at least cry, I got up and stomped around cursing, when two of Tifton's finest drove up. The only thing that the officer driving could say was, "Damn, I've never seen that before." Well, neither had I. Nor had I ever even heard of such an accident. At any rate, at that point, the police officers went into action, called their friend with the only wrecker in Tifton, and had me towed to the only auto dealership in town. I think it was a Ford dealership.

As soon as my pride and joy, now with a broken back, arrived at the dealership, the manager phoned the owner who was there in five minutes.

I think that it has been experiences like this that have taught me the difference between those individuals in life who practice compassion from those who simply discuss it, study it, or maybe preach it. Whether it was the police officers, the wrecker service, or the Ford dealership owner, all treated me as though we were life-long friends. After determining that there was not a rental car within one hundred miles of Tifton, and after my explanation that my truck and crew, none of whom knew where they were going, were probably 30 minutes down the road, the dealer muttered something about "aw hell, you take my car and I will just get Betty (...or whatever her name was...) to bring my pickup by for me this weekend." So after renting, at a very reasonable charge, the personal automobile of the Ford dealer and making arrangements to come back through Tifton the following Wednesday to check on my car, I was road-bound again heading toward Fernandina Beach, Florida, to catch the Greyfield boat, the Robert W. Ferguson, for its 4:00 p.m. run to Cumberland.

I don't think that Gene ever fully understood why I showed up in a different car. But somehow it didn't seem too important to me to explain what happened. However, Thornton Jr. and friends were infuriated that we were forced to leave the bikes in Tifton. As soon as we arrived at the dock we began to load the Island boat. And we got to Greyfield on Cumberland at about 5:30 p.m. After unloading Big Truck, and adding to the supplies the concrete blocks, lumber, and other building materials

The truck had picked up a large five-inch spider which was dangling no further than six inches from Geraldine's face.

which had been delivered to the Robert W. Ferguson, and some of which had already been moved to the Island, we began to load up every vehicle available to go north to MorrisTown.

Lucy Ferguson had promised the use of her two ton truck, Big Blue, which still ran but had neither lights nor windshield, and only the driver's side door would open. Also, there was available a farm tractor and flatbed trailer which we loaded with concrete blocks. There was another pickup truck, which also had no lights, which we loaded with lumber. Gene took his old panel truck which had one light and drove point. As we pulled out of Greyfield heading north on the main road, it became apparent to me that we had not included darkness into the equation, but we proceeded forward anyway. Before we got halfway to Stafford Plantation, it was pitch black dark. Each vehicle could barely see the one in front, the whole four vehicle train being led by a 1946 Dodge panel truck with only one light. At around 9:00 p.m., we decided to stop the slow train and take a rest. We had probably been averaging four or five miles per hour.

We stopped immediately south of what is now the Yankee Paradise Campsite. To cheer his troops, Gene came back to Big Blue. After Gene crawled up on the running board and gave Geraldine, riding shotgun, a cigarette, he struck a large wooden match to light it. Gene always carried large wooden matches rather than a cigarette lighter or a small book of matches. I think he probably liked the instant gratification – maybe it was a tad of testosterone. But whatever the reason, as soon as Gene lit the large match, everyone who was standing nearby, including Geraldine, noticed for the first time that the windshield-less, but quite tall cab on the two ton truck had picked up a large five inch spider which was dangling no further than six inches from Geraldine's face. The flare from the match probably accentuated the spider, and Geraldine totally freaked out. He had no intention of staying in the cab with that spider, but the shotgun door was jammed and you could only get through from the driver's side. And the driver was not moving from behind the steering wheel. Geraldine began screaming at the top of his lungs. He totally lost control of any rational behavior.

Instinctively, Gene stepped back from the window, and to all of our amazement, Geraldine dove head-first out the window. And the truck was probably five to six feet off the ground. There was a loud thud and groaning mixed with the screams. And to our further amazement – I personally was totally dumbfounded – Geraldine jumped up and began to run through the totally pitch black forest. We all winced as we heard thuds as Geraldine ran head-on into a tree, or when he fell, or ran over bushes, or whatever.

Gene was the first one to realize what was happening and made a dash after him. At about 50 yards into the woods, Gene tackled Geraldine and held him down until he came to his senses. (To say that Geraldine ever came to his senses may be overly complimentary, but Gene was able to slowly lead him back to the car.) Now, in addition to the side wound from the baseball bat, the black eye, and the swollen check bone, he had a bloodied nose, a twisted ankle, and what appeared to be an injured back. At this point, I am assuming that whatever liability insurance I had, its limits had been reached that evening, and the policy would be cancelled for the rest of my life. And Geraldine was whimpering in pain.

This, of course, was the period of the "70's" with all of its glories. Whether Geraldine was on LSD, mushrooms, peyote, or whatever, it was definitely more than the occasional Budweiser.

By 2:00 a.m., we had gotten over the second bridge north, the one at the Squawtown entrance. We only had about a mile to go. But as we were pulling over the third bridge, the one at MorrisTown, the bottom came out of the bridge and concrete blocks went everywhere. And the tractor and trailer did also.

This was before the National Park Service built the beautiful and strong wooden bridges of today. It was when we used sand on top of large culverts, and the sand had given way and the culvert collapsed. Unfortunately, the tractor and trailer were the second in the caravan, and we had to clean it up that night. By 5:00 a.m., we had the tractor and trailer back on the road and were finished loading the concrete blocks. Then we got Lucy Ferguson's Big Blue and the pickup truck over the culvert and pulled into the building area. We all stopped the vehicles and everyone either went to sleep in their vehicles or found something to sleep on and fell asleep. As the sun came up the next morning I could not get my eyes to open. Gene began to stir. Geraldine was feeling pretty badly. Gene woke everyone up and we began to plan the day.

Before anyone had much to say, Geraldine broke the silence by asking, "Where's the buildings?" Not understanding what he was asking, I asked him what buildings he was talking about. After the two others chimed in – Gene had little to say – it became apparent that Gene had sold the three on, in fact, going to Florida – Florida, with all its miniature golf courses, fast food franchises, carnival-like atmosphere, and bikini-laden beaches. As I began to explain to the three that we did not have that particular environment on Cumberland Island, the younger of the brothers made an observation that I have remembered my whole life. "Why in the living hell would anyone want to build a house in this God-forsaken place?" I had no ready answer for him, or at least one that he would have understood.

By noontime, Gene had his transit set up and was laying out the foundation of what was to become MorrisTown.

The boys had signed on for a minimum of three months. And it appeared for the first couple of days that they might work out. I left early Wednesday morning. Gene called via the ship-to-shore radio system then maintained by Greyfield, saying that the three had taken his only vehicle and driven the ten miles to Greyfield to buy some cigarettes with the understanding that they would return immediately. After spending Friday night alone in his tent and not hearing from the boys all day Saturday, Gene walked the ten mile distance down to Greyfield to find that they had abandoned all of their "stuff" at MorrisTown, had left his auto parked at Greyfield, caught the ferry to Fernandina, and were hitchhiking back to Floyd County, Georgia. I thought during the first of the conversation that Gene was throwing up his hands and himself escaping north. But he didn't. It was then that Andrew C. Ferguson, Mitty and GoGo's brother, stepped forward, as he did so often during the saga of MorrisTown, to save the day. Andy offered to help Gene, and it got him through this initial low point.

Andy was to perform that function several times throughout the building process. Gene would probably have been unable to finish the project had he not had Andy's support when needed.

MorrisTown was finished about a year later and served us well for years.

Gene Poole was always one to avoid strife, especially when the strife was with his wife, Inez. So it was not unusual that he waited until the last possible minute to tell Inez of the arrangements he had made to get her and their six kids off Cumberland Island after one of their periodic visits. Inez was the one who had just caused his tent to burn, with the subsequent loss of all his possessions. The fact that the fire was unintentional did not matter. Gene just did not want Inez or his family on the Island anymore. So he conveniently shifted the burden of their removal to me and some of my hapless office workers who had come with me to Cumberland for a pleasant summer weekend.

I knew that having Inez and his family endure such a long ride in a horse trailer in the heat of summer was of no special concern, or even bother, to Gene. Simply put, the Pooles were very, very tough customers. But when Gene told Inez of his plan, all hell broke loose. She screamed and yelled, cursed and spat. Of course, all her protestations were to no avail. In fact, Gene had already gone so far as to pack all of Inez's bags for her departure. By this gesture, he had made it unmistakably clear that on this day she would be back in Plainville before the sun had set.

I had tried in vain to steer clear of this whole arrangement. I had not succeeded when I told Gene that my vehicle was already full with my employees, and there was no room for Inez and the children in my car. His proposed solution to that was the open horse trailer. I flat out told him that neither my fellow passengers nor I were keen on having a family of seven riding behind us in a horse trailer.

Yet Gene would have it no other way — and I knew that no work would ever resume on my house until Inez and the children were off the Island. Besides, I knew that Gene needed to have some time to himself. Still, I couldn't help thinking that this ploy was a rather extreme way — even for Gene Poole — to go about a family's removal. But, thankfully, one of my female employees agreed to ride in the horse trailer with the Pooles, a gesture that seemed to please and placate Inez. Finally she was able to get herself and her brood inside the trailer, and the trip to Atlanta and Plainville was underway.

For some reason, the ferry that went to St. Marys on the Georgia side of the Island was not running that day, so we had to get to the mainland by way of Fernandina Beach on the Florida side of Cumberland. I did not think about it at the time, but this meant that — because we had a horse trailer behind us — we would have to stop at the Georgia agriculture inspection station when we crossed the state line near Folkston.

Even though this was much before the current concern over illegal aliens, I must admit that I was apprehensive about just what I would tell the officer at the inspection station about my "non-agricultural" cargo. When we stopped, he walked toward me with his pad and pencil already out. And before I could get any kind of explanation underway, he was already looking into the horse trailer.

The officer looked at Inez and her family and fell completely silent for a long time. Then he turned slowly and looked directly at me. Finally he looked back into the horse trailer, and again he stood silently for a while. Then he turned completely, looked at me for one final appraisal and said simply, "You don't see this type of load much anymore."

With that, the officer walked away, and the agricultural inspection was over. And so the Poole family, once again, was on their way back to Plainville.

Once I had left the inspection station, something told me that it would be prudent to set up some form of a signaling system between the horse trailer and my car. As soon as I could, I pulled over to the side on a long stretch of highway and got out a red handkerchief I remembered keeping in my truck. I gave this to the office worker who had volunteered to ride in the group and told her to wave it out of the trailer window whenever we needed to stop.

I must admit that I was apprehensive about just what I would tell the officer at the inspection station about my "non-agricultural" cargo.

This move proved wise. For just outside of Waycross, the red handkerchief went out. I hastily pulled the car over and when I was safely off the road, I ran back and looked inside the horse trailer. I quickly saw that one of the girls had a stream of blood running down her face, and another had blood pouring red from her nose. Inez was screaming her head off at her son, Lamar. Lamar was about five years old at the time, and Inez could not control him. He had a belt wrapped around his hand and had been beating his sisters with the buckle. My poor employee was terrified and simply could not believe what she had just seen. She had quite frankly never witnessed such behavior in her life.

I yanked Lamar out of the trailer. I shook him and set him in the other half of the trailer by himself. When he stopped struggling, I told Lamar that he had to behave himself for the remainder of the trip. I said this like I was talking to my hounds when they were acting crazy. Lamar understood my tone and language, because he always responded to firmness and control. He did not respect any sign of weakness at all. For the remainder of the trip, he did not leave his side of the trailer.

Lamar did not say a word to me, his sisters, or his mother all the way back to Plainville. When he got out of the car, his muteness continued, and he walked past me without uttering a sound. I watched him, his sisters, and Inez as they all walked into their house.

That was over thirty years ago, and it never really surprised me that Lamar Poole went on to lead a rough life. According to Inez, whom I hear from occasionally, he has been in and out of trouble most of his life. ✍

Very few natural treasures

have been saved in quite the

way Cumberland was.

Of Seines and Sharks

In looking back, I simply cannot understand why I wanted fish badly enough to go into the Atlantic up to my neck with a seine when the land temperature was hovering at about fifty degrees. However, Rick Ferguson, and a fellow who was helping with the cattle and horses which roamed the entire Island, and whom I knew only as "Cowboy," and I decided to drag a seine. We thought that some sea trout and mullet might be good for dinner.

We were on the Island with horses, gathering Miss Lucy's cows which, at the time, roamed from High Point at the north all the way to the jetties on the south end of Cumberland. We were rounding up the cows for shipment to market and inoculation. Prior to the ownership of most of the real estate by the National Park Service, Lucy had the use of the entire Island for her cattle operations. There are many stories of how the Park Service finally got Lucy to get her cows off of its property, but those are for another day.

It was Rick's suggestion to go seining as we sat on the porch of Greyfield one afternoon working on a bottle of Jack Daniel's. He had the seine, and Cowboy and I thought it sounded like great fun. We pitched the seine into the back of a four-wheel drive jeep which had been converted into a flatbed truck, grabbed some extra ice and cokes for the bourbon and headed for Stafford Shoals. This was my first time to pull a seine, and as far as I could tell Rick and Cowboy knew what they were doing. Without any direction, as we unloaded and straightened the netting, Cowboy headed directly into the ocean with the "deep end" of the seine. It became rather apparent that the expectation was that I too would go out into the water. It also became apparent to me that Rick had done this many times and clearly understood that his

job was to stay onshore, hold that end of
the seine, and tell everyone else what to do.

As I went deeper into the water, my craving
for fish slackened as soon as the cold waves
slapped up on my mid-section. I looked at
Rick from the corner of my eye, and he was
staggering with laughter.

By this time, Cowboy had the whole net out
into the ocean. The wooden pole holding
the end of the seine had about a fifteen-foot
rope tied to its bottom. That was to be the
line which I tied around my waist in order
to pull the seine along. Cowboy was to hold
the end of the pole on the floor of the ocean
in order to trap the fish. You really need
two people on the outside end of a seine.

Cowboy's six-foot-four, two hundred and
forty pound frame was handling the waves.
My five-foot-seven and a-half, one hundred
and forty-five pound body was not. And
I realized that I did not care if the fish
did go under the seine. There was simply

continued

no way that I could do anything against that tide. I was a human cork bobbing along. Then a wave hit me on the side of the face and I went under. I came up choking and coughing and was struggling with the outside of the seine when I heard Cowboy mutter something about a problem. I already understood that freezing and drowning was a problem.

I caught a glimpse of Cowboy's stone-white face out of the corner of my eye and realized that he was hollering. At that point, I saw the largest dorsal fin I have ever seen. The shark had been trapped in the net and was working its way out by probing the netting as it went deeper. Deeper meant our way — the deep end. I also realized that I was on the inside of the seine directly in the path of the oncoming, although sideways, shark. It was all I could do to keep my head above the water but I definitely could not get behind the seine.

The next thing I knew, I had grabbed onto Cowboy's back and was attempting to get onto his shoulders. I could hear him curse and laugh at the same time. Cowboy, engulfed by a human backpack, realized that I was in trouble, and let me hang on.

Cowboy managed to get behind the seine, and held the pole forward as the big shark turned and made a dash along the inside of the seine. As it went around, no teeth hit us but Cowboy got an eight-inch strawberry on his side where the skin of the shark whisked past. At this point, Cowboy and I had satisfied any desire to seine, and the shark had scared all the fish within shouting distance away from the net. I was utterly petrified, so we headed for shore.

By the time we got to shore, Rick had freshened both of our drinks and had our shirts and coats ready for us to slip on. He was busting a gut with laughter. I was not. When it became apparent to Cowboy that he had not lost any body parts, he also started laughing. It was only after I had finished the bourbon and coke that I found any humor in what we had experienced.

We went back to Greyfield in the jeep, checked the horses for the next day's long ride to the north end, and cooked steaks for dinner.

I have never since taken the outside line on a seine off Cumberland Island. ✒

Transmogrification

We laughed when this word showed up on a spelling bee for fourth graders. Then one day at Cumberland Island we learned its true meaning.

We are standing at the marsh's edge on a Sunday evening in spring. Sit here long enough and the stillest things reveal themselves slowly as living organisms. The old wet log on the bank becomes an eight-foot alligator, the driftwood at her side slides into the water: babies we could not distinguish at first glance.

The tiny blob of mud on the flat before us starts to move, tentatively at first then frantically, awakening millions of similar blobs and suddenly we are witness to a galaxy of miniscule drunken fiddler crabs emerging from their holes in the gray mud, bowing and shaking their one huge pincer-fist at interlopers.

The reeds in the salt marsh rattle (we are reminded of dry corn stalks in summer) and one startled redwing blackbird emerges, then another. They balance on the tall stalks and sing three lovely notes of summer coming.

Shadows along the new, bright green of palmettos at the forest's edge pull our gaze skyward. We are encircled by five wood storks descending to the creeks. Small white clouds become birds.

Tree trunks a half mile away transmogrify. What were predictable tree limbs become three wild horses slowly making their way out onto the mudflats.

Cumberland seems to be a professor teaching me that things are not always as they appear. And, at least for me, I am not who I was when I came here.

Is time always suspended on Cumberland Island?

A Spring Walk

Is time always suspended on Cumberland Island? My daughter, Vann, and I leave the house for the mile and a half walk to the beach on the South Cut Road and promptly lose ourselves in getting there. Not losing our way — we know it well as the path is old and familiar, one we share with the deer and raccoons and all of the people before us who have trodden the paths of Cumberland for thousands of years. But we lose ourselves and together become one more creature in the forest, shy and curious as the warblers that dangle in the Spanish moss. Silent except for the tread of our feet on the carpet of fallen oak leaves.

In the undergrowth less than fifteen feet away, a busy armadillo snuffles in the leaves oblivious to our presence. A raccoon emerges on a fallen log and sits staring. Red-headed woodpeckers swoop and dart into the canopy; a tiny unidentifiable warbler explores the green feathery resurrection fern on the side of a twisted oak branch above our heads.

We decide between us that the magnificent live oaks are old Zen masters; perfectly grounded in their purpose, peaceful, silent, strong, giving strength to others, taking only what they need to survive. Being their being. We have much to learn from them.

The path opens into a fresh water marsh, and there waiting for us is a mother alligator at the water's edge. She, like the oaks, sits wisely silent, an inscrutable sage basking in the spring sun, surrounded by six sleepy adolescents. Not even our shadows impress them into movement as we cross the marsh and stop to regard their world.

The dunes rise up out of the forest ahead. We can hear the ocean before we climb the last hill of sand and remember the purpose of our walk — the beach. The beach on a spring morning after a night of comfortable light rain. The beach in all its empty glory,

still quiet, inhabited only by a few gulls and a fan of sleeping terns nestled on the sand near the lapping water. Their orange bills are the brightest spot on the horizon. Otherwise, we are met with the beautiful browns and grays of the gulls and sands and the lazy waves of low tide. Sand dollars and coquina shells disappear and reappear in the surf, and we are transfixed by the myriad of color and pattern in the line of shells left by the tide. Vann picks up a perfect scallop shell, rubs it along her cheek, and drops it back onto the sand. She is hungry for every part of this morning. ✐♥

Sirens

I stared at the water puzzled after Sam and Boog Candler and I had opened the bottle of Merlot to have with our roast beef sandwiches. As we turned to look up the creek, we could not identify the source of the thrashing sounds. We were on the Perkins' dock at Squawtown sitting next to an overturned kayak which had probably not been used for several seasons. The dock has been on the Island for probably forty years and has a tin roof over it. It is the perfect place toward the north end of Cumberland to have lunch overlooking the creek and marshlands. We all stared over the marsh grasses bordering the creek to see what the incoming tide was bringing.

A half dozen or more dolphins, swimming in something of a formation, were splashing and making as much noise as possible. The creatures were utterly absorbed in what turned out to be a well-orchestrated game of fishing. On queue, and with the precision of a performing ballerina, the one on the far side zipped forward. With lightning speed, the dolphin surged ahead of the silvery glistening school of mullet located right ahead of him. Then, with a dive straight into the darting mass, he left the water with his body carrying up the mud bank no less than a hundred mullet. (At this point, the dolphin itself was on the bank about twelve feet from the water's edge.)

The sun flickered against the silver and white bodies of the thrashing mullet, as they struggled to find the safety and life of the water. The dolphin twisted and turned as he rolled and slid back into the water, catching mullet as he came down the bank. As his tail and flippers worked in unison, he slowly and effortlessly picked up and swallowed the individual mullet, gliding through the life sustaining ballet of sparkling light, water, and mud.

Then it was each dolphin's time to go on stage. One after another, they leapt onto the bank, then effortlessly slid and rolled back toward the water in a sliding feast of shining mullet.

We watched speechlessly as the last of the beached school were devoured by the dancing dolphins.

Before I was able to finish my glass of wine and mouthful of pretzels, the dolphins began their return trip. We had just finished discussing how the Greeks viewed dolphins as god-like beings, when we heard them coming in a playful mood down the creek. It had all seemed like a mystical experience, one that touched the soul more than the mind. Suddenly, Sam got up from our meal and softly slipped into the water from the floating dock. He was treading water in the middle of the creek when the aquatic troupe returned and surrounded him. For a moment, I thought we had lost Sam to the sea, enraptured by these magnificent creatures, sirens to a life beyond familiar ground.

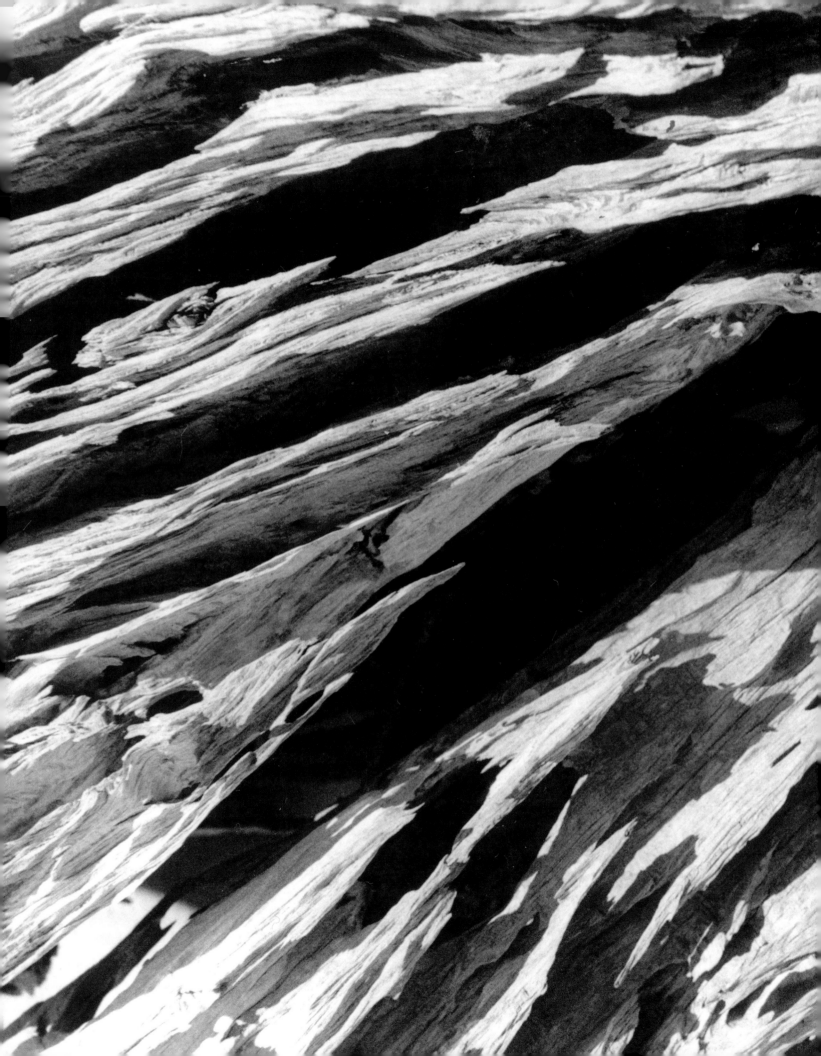

raccoons and all the people

before us who have trodden

the paths of Cumberland for

Bob and Dele Rischarde

The last time I remember seeing Bob was a year or so after Dele's death, and he was staying at their Ship House in Fernandina Beach, Florida. It was a replica of the shrimp boats which fish the Georgia coastline, except buried in the ground with the bow pointed toward the intracoastal waterway. It was late afternoon when I knocked on his door. The sun was in his eyes as it filtered through the screen, and I could see him talking on the telephone. I could not tell with whom he was speaking, but he cut the conversation short by saying, "There is a male Caucasian at my door, and I need to see what is going on."

Robert and Adele Hare Rischarde were two of the more beautiful people I have ever known. Both were always quite well dressed with something of a flare. Dele had long salt-and-pepper hair and a light brown face, resembling a Moorish Queen. She normally wore a black, perfectly proportioned, large shark tooth held by a band around her forehead. No one ever believed that Dele was just ordinary.

Bob, or so he told me, was born in Cave Springs, Georgia, to parents who were at the State of Georgia Deaf and Dumb School located there. He was shipped off to his aunt in Brunswick, Georgia, at age five, to be a runner for his aunt's business. In the period around the turn of the twentieth century, prior to cell phones and email, local "colored" whorehouses had to maintain a level of discreet communication between the madam and the clientele. Thus Bob started his life of trading and dealing. I never suspected Bob of anything morally wrong, but there were not many redcaps employed by Air France who had five homes scattered around the world and who only worked six months of the year. And it always seemed interesting to me that he was on a first-name basis with several of the presidents of Air France and at least one President of the United States.

He met President Carter while Mr. Carter was still governor of Georgia. The governor was visiting his friends Sam and Betsy Candler at High Point, the Candler family estate on the

96

north end of Cumberland. It seems that Mr. Carter happened upon Bob's house one morning about 10:00 a.m. when Bob was having his morning schnapps and was burning candles in his Buddhist garden after meditation. Mr. Carter was so taken with Bob that they became lifelong friends. Later, after Mr. Carter became President and invited Bob to Washington to stay at the White House, Bob told me that he was so excited about sleeping in Lincoln's bed that he wet the bed during the night.

Bob's small cottage is still located next to the AME Baptist Church at the north end of Cumberland. This small mystic church was the place selected by John F. Kennedy, Jr. for his marriage to Carolyn Bessette. Young John Kennedy visited Cumberland several times during his lifetime, before it was cut short by the airplane accident.

Bob Rischarde practiced the form of Buddhism known as Zen. His attempt to introduce me to Eastern philosophy in general, and Buddhistic theory in particular, came at a period of my life when it fell only upon Western ears. Although I found the philosophies to be beautiful, it was only later that I was able to internalize some of his way of thinking. At the time, I was able to get an inkling of insight into how his philosophies played out by watching the interchange between him and Dele. Mutual respect and admiration, coupled with verbal and physical support, seemed to be the foundation upon which they built the relationship which they enjoyed. At the time, I thought it unusual that Bob built a separate home, probably fifteen to twenty feet from his own little cabin, for Dele. "Respect" is what I remember him saying as to why he did it – something about the strength and independence of each of the two pillars of the partnership. In his other homes, such as the converted windmill in Portugal, or the brownstone in Harlem, or even the ship house at Fernandina, they lived together in the same dwelling. His feeling was that Cumberland was different, and two separate houses "felt" right. He also mentioned that he invited Dele over to his house often, especially at night.

When Bob died, primarily I believe from a broken heart upon losing Dele, he was buried next to her at a small graveyard on the north end of Cumberland. His body was brought to Cumberland in a casket on Greyfield's boat, the *Robert W. Ferguson*. Mitty Ferguson, the captain of the boat, along with several others, was dutifully carrying the casket off the boat onto the ramp. And, it was low tide. The ramp was as slick as grease and, as the first of the entourage stepped on the moss-covered planking, they went down. And, of course, with them went their end of the casket. After the usual embarrassment and guilt by each of Bob's friends who were temporary pallbearers, they finally realized that Bob Rischarde would have thought that being laid to rest in a casket, his body as entangled as a pushed rope, would have been a hilarious end to a wonderful life.

Bob Rischarde died in 1982. He was my friend. ✍♥

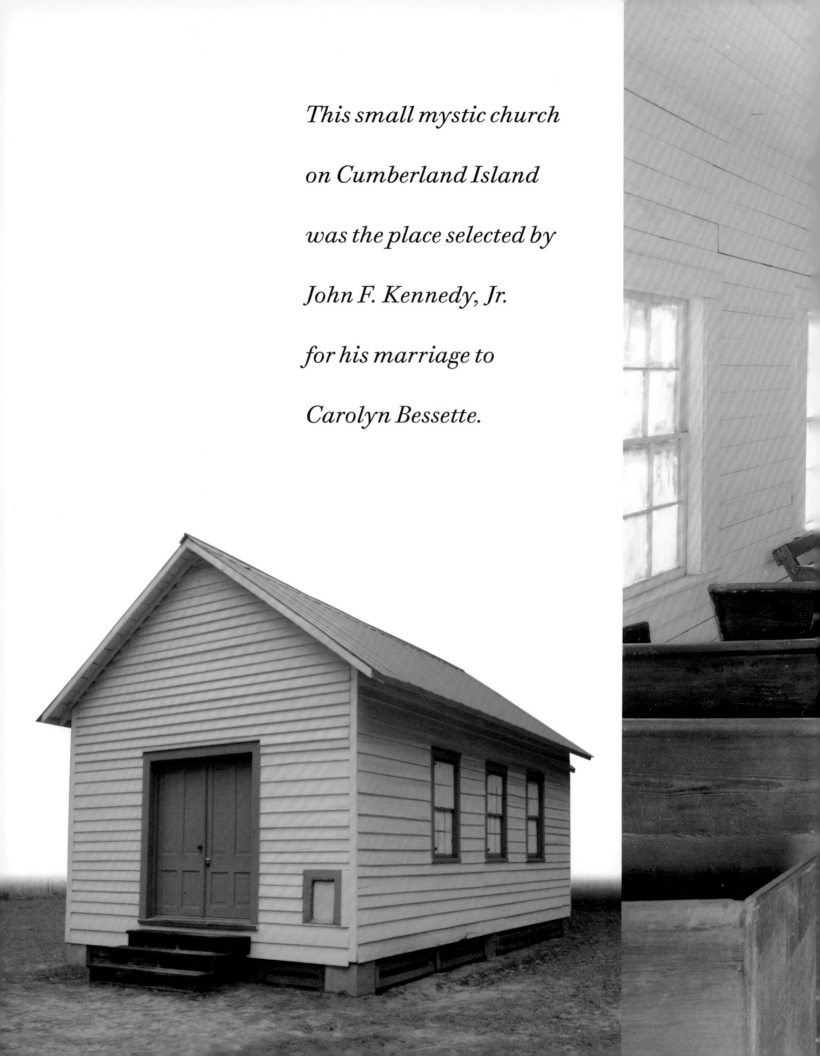

This small mystic church

on Cumberland Island

was the place selected by

John F. Kennedy, Jr.

for his marriage to

Carolyn Bessette.

Kennedy visited

Cumberland several

times during his lifetime,

before it was cut short by

the airplane accident.

Riley: Ace of Dogs

Cumberland Island, like all areas of great **wildness,** can be unforgiving. There are rules that have to be followed to survive, and this holds true for both man and beast. Though I have come to terms with Riley's death, knowing that he died doing exactly what he wanted to do, I still miss him terribly to this day.

I was on Cumberland with my son, Scott, and a few friends and, of course, Riley. Riley was a Jack Russell terrier with an uncanny ability to get his way. He and I were the best of friends, and we got along famously as long as we let one another live his own life. He and I had many hours together both on my farm and on Cumberland, but I always thought Riley just sort of tolerated my human activities, knowing deep-down that his dog activities were the more significant. He enjoyed riding in a milk crate on the back of my motorbike and quite often I found him sitting there, waiting for me to take him for a ride. He knew I'd always come eventually.

We walked and rode and explored the Island and its beaches together, though I suppose he covered a lot more territory than I will in my lifetime. His greatest passion was taunting and doing battle with the Island's raccoons. I gave up on trying to break him of this habit. It was as if he had been put on this earth to dedicate his life to limiting the coon population on the Island, and his ferocity was astonishing. I learned early on to stay out of the fray and let Riley and the raccoons make their own rules and decisions about existence.

It was a steamy evening in late summer. We were sitting around the dinner table talking late as we often do at the Island. Silhouetted against the horizon on the

ke all areas of great wildness, can be unforgiving.

marsh was the familiar sight of Riley and a raccoon in mortal combat. I thought nothing of it and continued to converse with my guests. Riley, a canine Bonaparte if ever there was one, was all over a particularly large raccoon that slowly backed and clawed and fought his way closer to the water's edge. Scott pointed out that things were getting unusually heated in the fight but I really didn't think Riley could ever lose and so I continued the dinner table discussion while the sun set and the tide began to come in. This, of course, was Riley's Waterloo. The coon knew well the water was rising and let Riley play his hand. Fur and blood flew. All the while that raccoon worked his way slowly into the water, taking Riley in all his fury with him. The next thing we knew Riley was in over his head, probably exhausted but refusing blindly to give up the fight. It was too late when I realized what had happened: the raccoon had led Riley to his death by drowning.

We spent the next day preparing a burial for this amazing dog. Friends prepared a headstone and a cross, I opened a few bottles of my best champagne and we toasted Riley. He's buried out on the point in the marsh where his ghost continues to taunt raccoons at every sunset, and I am humbled over and over by the closeness of death on Cumberland. It was the one time this brilliant little dog forgot the rules of Cumberland Island: The tides are inexorable; the pull of death is always near at hand.

Riley was with me during the period when I moved from my childhood understanding of animals to the one I have today. I, like probably most other farm boys, grew up believing that only humans had souls. Other beings may have had many attributes, but no soul. I am not sure how far I have gotten in my belief that all beings, just like humans, have souls, but I can say that if I have one, so did Riley. My whole life has been a conflict between being a child of the Age of Reason, with its nagging agnosticism, and the belief that something more exists in the universe than just the power of me. My acceptance of the belief in a universal intelligence occurred during the period of my life with Riley. I don't know if he had anything to do with it.

Witnessing a Hurricane

hen my son, Thornton, Jr., was about six years old, he and I were house sitting at Greyfield for a week. Robert Ferguson had just passed away, and everyone was off to Massachusetts for the service. A hurricane moved through – not a huge hurricane, but one dramatic enough to remain in detail in my mind for thirty years.

The eye came right over the Island and when we realized the storm wasn't going to be grand enough to hurt the house, we decided to feel as much of the storm as possible. We donned yellow foul-weather gear, grabbed snorkeling equipment, and jumped in the jeep and headed to the beach for the second-blow that was sure to follow the eerie quiet of the eye's passing. I can still remember the absolute silence of those minutes between blows; not a bird's smallest twitter, no cries of gulls, just utter silence from the livestock Lucy kept. None of the normal racket of everyday life on the Island could be heard, as if everyone was equally awed by the storm and respectful if its powers.

The storm that raged on the beach that afternoon was like nothing I have ever witnessed. We had to wear our goggles and even use the snorkels just to breathe because the sand was so thick in the air. It moved like a sheet of liquid sandpaper down the beach, burnishing any portion of flesh left uncovered. We watched as entire dunes formed and disappeared and re-formed again. I remember thinking my son looked like a small astronaut in yellow on the surface of Mars or the moon. We could lean into the wind at 45-degree angles, defying gravity, occasionally being lifted a few inches off of the ground by its force. God's own voice screamed through us that day; we were deafened by the howls and thrashing of water, sand and blackened air. Walls of sea foam formed off of the surface of the raging surf and engulfed us periodically. I would lose Thornton in the foamy white momentarily, then suddenly his small body would slice through the wall and I could catch the flash of his white teeth in an ecstatic grin of a six-year old alive and thrilled by the elements of the firmament.

The only thing that is certain about a hurricane is that change is coming. Trees are covered, not to be seen again for years, and then only as skeletal remains of once living organisms. Later I was thinking that maybe security for me has come with the knowledge that with life, there will be change. Rather than fearing it — with change, I have new challenges to see what opportunities develop.

I can still remember the

absolute silence of those

minutes between blows;

not a bird's smallest

twitter, no cries of gulls,

just utter silence from the

livestock Lucy kept.

The Hunt

Fox hunting is a winter sport on Cumberland Island. This timetable is primarily for the benefit of the horses. Since the horses we use in fox hunting are brought down to Cumberland from North Georgia, they are not accustomed to the hoards of insects that invade the Island during the spring and summer months. Cumberland's bug population goes down with the arrival of winter and its killing frosts, so both animals and humans can enjoy a respite from their stings and bites.

On crisp winter mornings, we begin the hunt with stirrup-cups of sherry or port. Horses have been brought in from the mainland for the hunt, and, on the Island, twenty-five or thirty foxhounds stand at the ready. Prior to this, something we call the "laying of the line" has taken place. This is the

continued

The Nature of Hounds
& Hunts

Hounds are probably the most well developed "smelling machines" on the planet. On Cumberland, they have been used historically to hunt foxes, raccoons, and hogs. The types of hounds used in each of these hunts are quite different. In fox hunting, only the finest of pack hounds (team players) are employed. No prima donnas here. A coordinated chase is the centerpiece of this daytime sport, so you need a skillful pack of thirty to fifty hounds that functions as the ultimate hunting team. This pack is the direct DNA result of its predecessor — the wolf pack. However, when you are hunting raccoons at night, you need only one or two hounds that can hunt alone and function individually. These are good individual hounds, but not the pack hounds of fox hunting. When wild hogs are your game, you again need a hound's nose to locate the quarry. But hog dogs must be fierce fighters as well, because the tusked prey they attack can easily rip them apart. For this reason, hog hounds are frequently bred with pit bulls, a combination that pairs the hound's excellent nose with the pit bull's tenacity.

While fox hunting does not entail the death of any animal, both coon and hog hunting are blood sports. This simply means something gets killed, and it is not always the prey. A hound will normally grab a hog by the leg, or maybe on the neck or ear. The hunters must then rush to the site of the attack and quickly shoot the hog in the head if it is a boar. This is dangerous work. Hounds can get their stomachs ripped to pieces, and the hunters can get gored. The boars have tusks and can savagely impale a hound or human with these lethal and potent weapons.

I first began hunting raccoons as a child on my family farm. Later, when I was on Cumberland, I would go out at night with some of Lucy Ferguson's employees. They were simple country men who were born on farms or came to Cumberland Island from the nearby Okefenokee Swamp. When they hunted it was for food and not just for sport, and I learned much about hounds from these hard working individuals.

continued

dragging of a scent, or line, for the hounds to follow. This is done on Cumberland because there are no foxes on the Island, or at least I have never seen or heard of a fox there. So, naturally, the hounds must have something to follow.

These "fox-less" hunts usually last for around a week. Twenty-five or more friends come and sleep all over MorrisTown. They sleep on sofas and chairs, in halls and on the floor. Some of the early arrivals actually manage to claim a bed. No matter. We all enjoy ourselves immensely.

Fox hunting is not a blood sport. It is simply a chase where no killing is involved. Nevertheless, emotions run high. In the bracing cold weather, you can see the horses' breath snorting out of their nostrils like fog. Below them, the foxhounds eagerly sniff the winter air. No one, not even the huntsman, knows the precise location or route the drag will take across the Island. The humans are well fortified with sips of sherry or port and are perched atop their mounts like sailors in the crow's-nest of a ship looking ahead for land. So we are off, running pell-mell through woods, marsh or beach — wherever the hounds lead us.

After the run, the hounds are exhausted and the horses are soaked in sweat. The humans are equally spent, and we all head for the hunt breakfast, which is a historical term we now call lunch. Afterwards, we take a rest and then get up to explore the Island or look for any foxhound who may not have returned with the pack. By nightfall, we are all back at MorrisTown — ready

and eager to relive the day's events over dinner and whiskey and prepared to resume the next day's hunt in the morning.

For all of us — hounds, horses, and humans — these are good times. I like to imagine that if foxes were plentiful on the Island, they would enjoy these romps as much as we all do. Probably the foxes would outrun us all. ✒

Hounds & Hunts

continued

The dogs are never petted except by their owners — which is characteristic of people who hunt hounds. They are bred and raised to be fierce, and this toughness is the center of their being. No rural houndsman wants his good hog dog coming up for a pat on the head by someone else. These hunters hunt to live, and hunting is serious business to them. They feed their families better by hunting, and none of them ever wants a hunting dog to be a pet.

When I used to bring my Harlech Hounds, a pack of "Old English" tricolor fox hounds, to hunt on the Island, we would get my good friend Henderson Wright to come along. Henderson was called the "lean, mean killing machine." He drove a four-wheeler and prided himself on not being a horseman. When we would hunt the hounds during the day, Henderson would go into the woods and get us anything we needed to feed them. If we wanted two or three hogs to feed to the dogs that night, he would always find them, and his fire was ablaze by late that afternoon and the meat was already cut up. Over the open fire, Henderson would just sear slices of wild hog and toss them to the hounds while the meat was still sizzling. They literally would go crazy as they dove into this feast and ate their fill with ravenous delight.

Whenever possible, we fed the hounds raw meat. Whenever a horse, cow or farm animal died near my farm, the farmer would bring the carcass over for the hounds to eat. They gorged themselves, and in a week everything — bones, intestines, organs, and even hair and eyeballs — would be totally devoured.

I often tell my friends this is the way I want them to dispose of my remains. No burial. No cremation. Not even a flaming Viking ship asea for me. Just lay me out and call for the Harlech Hounds. For me, ending up in the stomach of these wonderful hunting companions would be the finest funeral rite this side of the Atlantic.

This brings me to an observation I have made. After asking people over the years what they considered to be the worst form of death, invariably I get the answer of being eaten alive. Other than the occasional big bad wolf stories that we heard as children, there is not much discussion during this period of history of humans being devoured. Obviously that was not the case 20,000 years ago. When humans were just as much the hunted as the hunter, the fear of being eaten must have been with us minute by minute. Very seldom have I thought that having my body demolished in an interstate wreck, or being crushed by a piece of heavy equipment, or some other more common form of very painful, premature death would be the worst way to go. Invariably, I come back to the "eaten alive" alternative.

These early observations in my life caused me to be skeptical of the claims in the 70's and 80's by the American intellectual community that most all behavioral patterns of humans were the product of our environment and not being "in the blood" so to speak. DNA research during the later part of the 20th century seems to have validated many of the observations that our thinking may be "hard-wired" more than our society would like to think. Otherwise, we would be much more afraid of a Peterbilt than an alligator. *L♥*

A Home Built on Trust

robably the dream to live on an island has tantalized humans forever.

So....I began to build, again!

My thought was to provide a sanctuary for each of my children. It was also to provide a place for someone to live part-time to look after the place.

Martin Gillette, my good friend, became the caretaker for MorrisTown. When he is not rendering decisions as the Judge of the Probate Court of Camden County, Georgia, he is on Cumberland repairing all of the things that happen on an Island, and living in an apartment at MorrisTown. It is hard to see how anyone could do a better job and be a better friend.

The original plans were to have the additional four suites attached to the existing house. The old MorrisTown had a country cottage design with a front porch large enough for rocking and a screened back porch which held a large hand made table with benches. The idea was to build the new suites as a part of the existing dwelling.

After a preliminary design was prepared for each suite, and the total size of the addition was determined, Martin signed on to the project of getting the house renovated. His job was getting the supplies from the mainland to the Island. Transportation is no small item when building a house on an Island. If the carpenters run out of nails or are a bundle of shingles short, there is no hardware store to send a worker to buy more. It is a challenge, bordering on an unmitigated hassle, to build a home on an Island.

Well, the first thing that Martin set out to accomplish was to select the right person to construct the house. We discussed several of the builders who operate "over on the mainland," and they simply did not feel right. Finally, he introduced me to Onie Lee Butler

and I was sold. Onie Lee and his two brothers, Arthur and Clifton (also known as "Wenchie"), were the employees of Butler Construction Company of Kingsland, Georgia. Onie Lee ran the show. Onie Lee once told me that he only liked to employ his family members – they were the only ones he could really trust.

Although we began the project with Onie Lee having a set charge for each part of the construction, Martin soon realized that the system simply made no sense when building on an Island. If Onie Lee was able to come in under the time which he estimated for a given project, he would receive a bonus. However, if he ran over the time, he would simply quit the job because he did not have enough money to fund any shortfall. Therefore, it should not have been a surprise when one day Martin called me to tell me that we should go on a "straight time" basis with Butler Construction Company.

You can imagine my wincing when Martin suggested that I pay Onie Lee and company on a time rate for work performed on an Island with absolutely zero supervision. After swallowing hard, I gave Martin the green light and off we went.

They say that reward tends to follow risk. Well, when it comes to Onie Lee Butler and the members of his family, taking that risk, resting totally on trust and integrity, was one of the best decisions I have ever made. I have gained from the Butlers a new level of trust and expectation of things going right, rather than things going wrong. Throughout the construction, not one time did I feel that Onie Lee, Arthur, and Wenchie were not giving their all, week after week, even though there was no one there to supervise them. Onie Lee has helped me in moving from one level of working with people to another.

When Martin signed on for the journey, he had in mind that the whole project would probably take nine months, possibly a year, and then only if we ran into some particular problems. Nowhere in his wildest imagination did he assume that it would take three years and three months to get the renovation finished.

For three years, Martin could be seen in the afternoon running out of the courthouse, slinging his judicial robe over the back of the Chippendale antique chair in his office, sliding into old and torn blue jeans and boots, and scurrying to meet Onie Lee and company when they were arriving at the Mainland dock after a day's work on Cumberland. After getting a list of the supplies needed for the next day, and ironing out any wrinkles encountered during the day, he would make a mad dash to Choo Choo Lumber Company in St. Mary's or Home Depot in Brunswick before their closing time. For three years and three months, Martin would have in Onie Lee's boat the following morning the necessary supplies so that before the sun was very high in the sky, the construction company was on its way to the Island for another day. To my recollection, except for one day when the storms raged so great that no one would get in a small craft, Onie Lee and his family crew could be seen with a small rooster tail behind his boat heading to Cumberland Island for a day's work. And on every one of those days, there were supplies and material for him on the job.

As I said, I had obtained written plans for the addition. It was to encompass four apartments, each with a similar floor plan. After we got the basic structure built, Onie Lee began to scratch his head over how to tie the roofs together so that it was one building. It was during the "tie-in" period that we set aside all of the written plans and began to improvise on a bi-weekly basis. The last time I remember seeing anything written was about six months into the project, and Onie Lee was verifying some dimensions. For two years and nine months afterwards, no written plans existed. However, what I did not understand was that they were all in Onie Lee's head. He knew what needed to be done and slowly began the process of doing it.

The breezeway in the middle of the house was my idea. I wanted an open bar area — a pub if you will — so that I could use the bar top hand carved from a single piece of wood by my friend, Jay McLauchlan, of Gloucester, Massachusetts. Jay was Lucy Ferguson's former son-in-law, being formerly married to Lucy's daughter, Cindy. Also, I wanted to use two antique Doric columns, which had come from a stately home in Rome, Georgia, which had been torn down to make way for the expansion of the local Catholic Church. I had owned the home for some time and wanted to save it, when it fell into a bajillion pieces as we attempted to move it to my farm in North Georgia. So, I kept the columns instead. Thornton Jr., and his wife Ann, Scott, and Vann each designed the inside of their particular apartment the way they liked it.

And finally, we were finished. But I did not know what to do with the old portion of the house which now looked like the stepchild of MorrisTown.

When no one came up with a better suggestion, we decided to build a new house on top of the old MorrisTown. After completely refitting the old house with new windows, doors, etc., and being unable to get the roofline to look right, we built another roof on top of the existing one. The end result is that the old MorrisTown has completely changed, and it now appears to be a wing of the whole house.

The tower protruding from the center of the house up four stories was the brainchild of my friend, Charles Nail. It breaks the house up visually and gives it a part of its distinctiveness.

After about a year into construction, I found myself moving my legal residence to Cumberland Island. It seems to have been a proper thing for me to have done.

The Butler family is unlike many black families that the American press would expect for us to assume exist. I understood early in our relationship that Onie Lee believes in hard work, honesty and integrity, and the free enterprise system. However, when his son, Alvin, gave me a Christmas present of a statue honoring the confederate battle flag, I was somewhat surprised. Alvin simply referred to it as "our" flag. I later found out that he had bought two at the same time, a "get two for the price of one" sale, so that he would have one in his home on the mantle in his living room.

The old house at MorrisTown was a place to sleep, eat, and entertain. Although we had a back porch and often ate there, it was, in reality, a home intended for "inside" living. The revised MorrisTown is quite the contrary. It is encircled by a large porch with French doors opening onto it in several places. I found myself constantly gravitating toward the southwest corner of the house, putting dining tables there, sofas and lounge chairs, and finding myself, without realizing it, actually living outside on the porch more than inside the house. It faces the marsh, with a creek on the left, and with large live oaks all around. Later, in studying the Tao, I happened upon the original philosophy of feng shui.

As I began to read about this mystery of feng shui, it began to unfold to me that I had built my house in probably the most energy-conducive location I could have selected. The southwest corner of MorrisTown seems to satisfy most all of the principles enunciated in the Taoist philosophy of feng shui. My original notion that it had been a very fortunate coincidence has subsequently given way to other explanations. ✍

MorrisTown

CUMBERLAND ISLAND

CAMDEN COUNTY, GEORGIA

To my children on December 25, 2002

I have rebuilt MorrisTown in order to provide a private suite for each of you, to help you appreciate the unique gift we have on Cumberland. This is a very special place to me. I believe that the portion of my life which I have spent on the Island has changed the way I view the world. It has helped me immeasurably in my own journey to the place I find myself today.

We have this land because of Coleman ("Coley") Carnegie Perkins. Of my children, only Thornton knew Coley. I wish everyone had known him. He was an extraordinary man.

My dream in rebuilding this home is for us all to enjoy it as a family. Each of us will have our own individual space, and our meals and evenings together. I have designed it so that it will be a way to hold us all together when each of you has children and grandchildren. I hope that it will be a place to accommodate everyone.

Living within the natural setting of Cumberland, on an island, with no close neighbors has, I feel, helped me in sorting our many of the issues with which I have dealt in my life. It has helped me to replace indifference with love. Have compassion govern my life rather than withdrawal. Cause forgiveness to be stronger than resentment. Risk more rewarding than fear. And remind me that adventure has a higher yield than safety, and that passion has more rewards than reluctance and hesitation.

Up until now, the place in this world that has provided me the most openness in my growth in these areas has been Cumberland. It is my laboratory for life, the lens through which I see my soul. It seems to provide me the properly honed bifocals to help me see the good rather than just the OK in life. To see the extraordinary rather than just the everyday. To feel the now rather than fretting over yesterday and tomorrow.

These are just a few of the reasons why I have provided a home for you on Cumberland. If you are able to take away a fraction of what I have gotten from the Island, I will consider my efforts a success.

Cap'n John

Cumberland Island is the home of eccentric characters. None was more so than Captain John Townsend.

Perhaps my fondest memory of "Cap'n John" goes back to the late sixties when I had gone down to the Island in the winter to do some duck hunting. I was staying at one of the small houses at Greyfield for two weeks, and I needed to go down the river to Fernandina to get groceries and supplies. Cap'n John captained the Island boat, The Dungeness, which was a converted shrimp boat serving as a ferry service for both passengers and cargo and plied the waters between Cumberland and the mainland. Hollywood could not have typecast a better or more colorful old salt. Cap'n John always sported a four or five day stubble and unkempt khaki pants and shirt. This particular morning was a cold winter one, and so Cap'n John was wrapped up in a thick, faded navy blue jacket. Perched in the captain's

cabin with his hands on the wheel, the Captain looked like a man who could face anything. With his cigarette and captain's cap, he could have come out of any Winslow Homer seascape.

Because it was so cold that morning, I was riding in the captain's cabin with a fellow passenger, Margaret McDowell, one of Lucy Ferguson's two daughters. Cap'n John and everyone else called her Retta. Retta and I both loved to hear him talk on the radio. Although he was white, Cap'n John had something of a "Gullah" accent that was also quite guttural.

Even today, I can still hear his voice. He had a ship-to-shore radio, and he knew all the shrimpers and watermen up and down the river. On this bitterly cold day, he would call and jokingly taunt them as he passed their houses on the water. They should be out on the water with him, the good captain would tell them – not at home with their wives drinking coffee. Then you could hear the men and their wives laughing in the background, and soon Cap'n John would laugh and smile at us and continue down the river. Just these friendships and the water were his rewards. He was a man dedicated to his craft, and he loved the Island where he had lived for a great deal of his life. Captain John Townsend was simply a man well suited to what he did, and no one could do it better. ✒♥

Finding Forever in the Moment

It was cool and crisp at daybreak that morning. The dusty thermometer in the barn read 53 degrees. GoGo and her friend, Christina Haig, were coming to ride with me that morning. Both are good riders. GoGo, a granddaughter of Lucy C. R. Ferguson, knew how to handle a horse. Her grandmother raced on the mainland at the Camden Jockey Club. She took on Camden County's best riders, mostly male, and as best as I am told, seemed to have held her own. It is hard for me to imagine Lucy ever not holding her own. GoGo's father, Rick, and I drove cattle by horse down the Island, fifteen-plus miles of it, in and out of Palmetto bushes, thistle and vines, to carry the cattle to market on the mainland. She came from good riding stock. Christina was an actress from New York City. She had previously visited the Island, and GoGo, several times.

I was having a hard time catching the horses that morning – no one wanted to cooperate. Dar-es-Salaam always picks up my moves. She is a big tall chestnut thoroughbred mare, seventeen hands, and I always wonder why I keep her when she does not want to cooperate. She has the innate ability to tell me in advance when I need to cool it. She was doing that this morning.

After finally catching the horses, feeding a bit of sweet feed, and leaving the girths loose for final tightening right before mounting, I had the horses ready to go when I saw the Jeep drive into the yard.

GoGo was riding Jack (a/k/a Stonewall Jackson) my thoroughbred hunter jumper. Christina was on Sandy, a gray Arab hunter.

We headed out of MorrisTown along a road covered with deer tracks, the markings of bobcats and raccoons, with the ground torn up by wild boar looking for underground morsels. During the day, we came upon Bunkley Trail, a two-mile mystical stretch of trail which was no more than three feet wide and was tunneled from the canopy of scrub oak, vines and sassafras. GoGo, who was leading the way, leaned around in the saddle smiling and dug her heels into Jack's ribs. It was clear that he was ready to go, but it was not so clear that I was ready for Dar to bolt also.

After grabbing Dar's mane with one hand while holding the reins as best I could, we began to enter a whole new space of life. As our speed increased, the assumption of my ever returning home with both arms and legs decreased. However, as we sped up, I found myself living with the moment. The faster we went, the slower my mind moved. At one point, with mud splattering across my face and body from Christina's gelding, I looked at the wall of vegetation to my side and could almost see each square inch of it. It was as though the world had stopped with me going as fast as I possibly could on the back of a racehorse.

Time simply stopped. Noise subsided. A strange wave of silence engulfed me. I looked to my right and saw an individual leaf. Then another. And another. I was operating in a slow-motion time zone, a world of no yesterday or tomorrow. A reality of now. This moment. I understood that I had broken through some form of barrier which is based upon a human perception of time. As I was holding a handful of mane, with my head lying on the neck of my mare, hooves flying, mud splattering, I began to think about cavalry charges. I thought about a particular charge. It was British. I do not know who the enemy was. I felt myself swooping down on a foe, slashing, maiming, destroying. After a period of time, I do not know how long it was, I was back to the present and had lost my temporarily induced sensation of slow-motion.

I did not mention my vision to either GoGo or Christina. I do not know whether I was having some form of past-life regression, or possibly some genetic remembering from an ancestor, or maybe nothing more than a daydream. However, it seems significant, even a decade later. I think about it often.

Time simply stopped. Noise subsided.

A strange wave of silence engulfed me.

Love's Evolving Power

The day was cold and wet with rain. Coming down in cloudbursts, it poured relentlessly from my hat and down into my face, completely soaking my breeches and leather boots. All this was accompanied by a howling north wind that ripped the sand from the beach and blew it violently across the shore. The severity of it impressed me immensely. I liked it. I liked it very much.

I was glad that you were there with me. Standing with you in the unforgiving elements, I looked at you and I knew that I wanted to kiss you, to touch your cheek, your neck. I wanted to kiss you all over. In the fierce cold of that day I could only think of how I wanted to make you warm. I wanted us to lie on a rug in front of the fireplace and drink warm Spanish wine together.

It is special in life to be with someone with whom I do not need to speak. Communication always comes in many different forms. We can look into each other's eyes and know how we each feel. Touch, sight, taste — these are the fundamental senses that tell me what I need to know. But when we do talk, it is about meaningful things. Feelings I have. That you have. I see a tear in your eye. With the strength you have to be vulnerable comes my own response. My eyes become misty. I feel you. I feel what you are feeling. I am inside you. And for one fleeting moment, I am you. We are fused. One. A single mass of protoplasm, glued together by the power of the soul.

I look at you. Your face reflects experienced innocence. You project a form of power with your eyes, your mouth. The way you look at me with your large eyes. You stare into my eyes. You don't look aside after a comfortable second and a half expires. It is now two, three, four, five, ten seconds. You are still looking into my eyes. You show strength in ways that are meaningful. You turn me on. You know how I gravitate toward power and energy. You are really not thinking. It is reaction. The watery eyes again. My reaction.

We are back in the house. You lean toward me and I smell your hair. You have moisture from the rain on your forehead. I lick it off. You taste good. Like your scent, it stays with me. It is distinct, different; it is you. It makes me feel wild, untamed, from another period of history, to experience you. I nose into your stomach. I breathe heavily, taking in all of you. Was that an actual growl that I just made? What was that sound? It was guttural, from much earlier in the development of the human species.

I feel unrestrained by these relatively new rules of human conduct. Rules that only started a few thousand years ago. I feel that only a few things matter — food, fire, apparel for my body heat…my body heat…yes, and the inner urge to find body heat. Your body heat. Next to mine. And the taste of your mouth, your neck, your arms. I feel you breathe. Faster now. Now much faster. I feel primal — from another period, from another age. I am not of the now. I am of the before.

Why do I elect to live in today's rules, mores developed by other individuals? I rebel — yet still I must live during the day in a camouflaged acceptance of modern reality. But I am different — very different. I think differently, I feel differently. Why did I have to force back a tear when I looked into the sad face of the counter girl at Starbucks? Yet I could direct a military charge that would take many lives of people I know and love. So, unsurprisingly, I find myself moving from the mainland to an offshore island. To settle there, not merely physically — but emotionally and spiritually as well. It is a place apart. I am left there being who I am.

Who am I?

Living on the Island, I come to know so much more about myself than before. I like myself better. The types of people I like seem to be with me more.

My arms are secure around your body. I am careful to make sure that I am tender, warm – that I provide only pleasure. I am the conduit between fantasy and ecstasy. I am not conscious of what I am doing. I am just doing. You move with more force. I anticipate each sound and move, and I am moving faster and faster – I am with you. A long scream. Was that also from another period? Was it the same as when we lived in caves? Are you feeling the same as I am feeling? Did you even hear my deep growls?

You are quiet now. No movement. Just a flinch and some shuddering now and then. I do not want to remove my lips from you. It has now been a long time. Time? It

stands still. I know no time. Only feelings. It is good. It is very good. It is very, very good. It is now. It is not yesterday or tomorrow. It is at this instant in time. This moment in the history of the world. Eleven billion, seven million, two hundred forty-eight thousand, three hundred and sixty-two years since the creation of time. No, not just that, but also eight months, thirteen days, three hours, thirteen minutes and five seconds since then. Now. This is all that counts. Now. It is what matters. It is what is, what has brought us to here. The now.

You kiss my face. You are warm. My face is next to yours. We talk about quantum physics, coffee, Nepal, how much I like being with you.

I brought you here in order to help me get to know you. I am glad I did. I am beginning to see and feel you inside and out. Naked and unclothed – spiritually, emotionally, intellectually, and physically. ✍♥

It is my

laboratory

of life, my

Garden

of Eden.

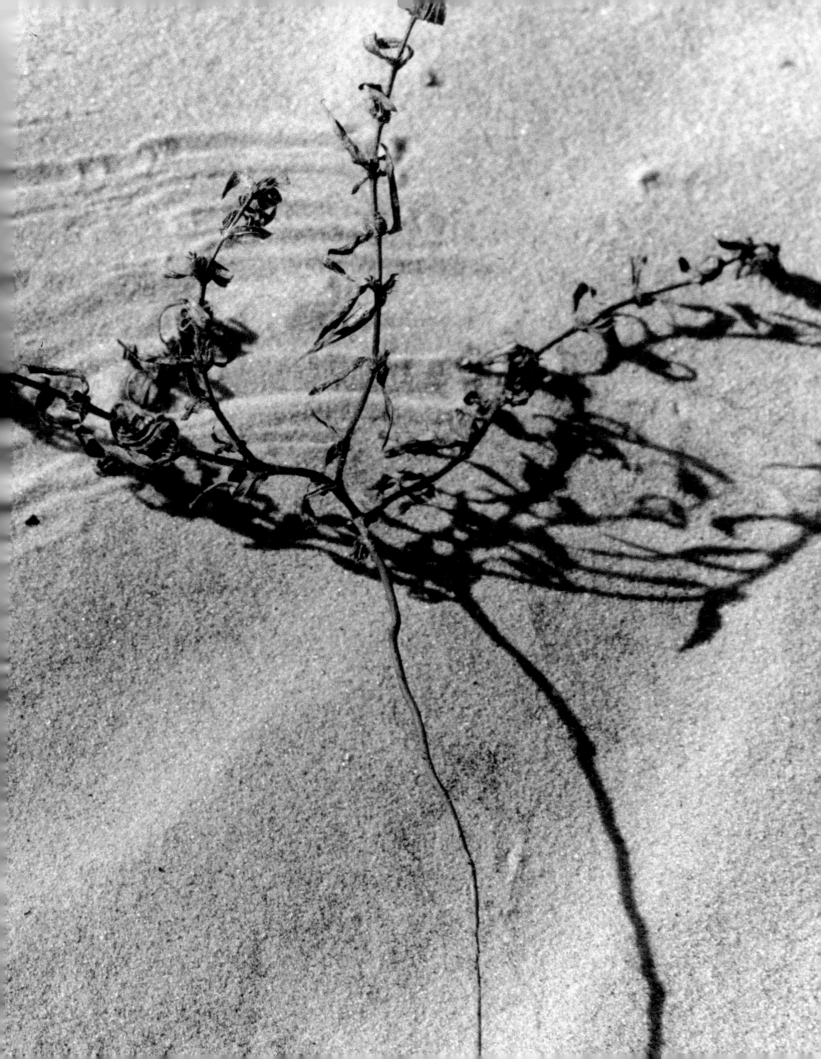

The Gift of Wonder

I **never thought about Cumberland Island** having much similarity with equatorial Africa until the Pygmies came over for a visit. I did not personally witness their arrival, but GoGo Ferguson has a videotape of it and, every time I see it, I am completely fascinated.

As it happened, the Pygmies were on a tour of America as members of a show that featured their tribal dances. They were somehow involved with White Oak Plantation, which is just across the river from Cumberland where, during the 1990's, Mikhail Baryshnikov had a dance studio. GoGo heard about it and went over to see the newly arrived Pygmies, video camera in hand.

She convinced them to take a boat to Cumberland Island. The Pygmies were delighted with their new surroundings as soon as they got onshore. Instantly these small Africans were attracted to the Island's palmetto trees, and you could see their glee as they ran among them with complete abandon. Surely something about these subtropical bushes must have reminded the Pygmies of their homeland, because GoGo's videotape shows them hugging the boughs and vividly waving the palmetto fronds in the air like flags.

And, when they saw the Atlantic beach, they became totally ecstatic. They ran and frolicked in the waves like children. Being only three to four feet tall, they even looked like small children. Watching them on tape, I was taken with their wardrobe — such an amalgamation of clothes and style. The Pygmies would don the most colorful garments, which they probably had assembled from all the ragtag shops they found on their tour. Stripes and solids were completely mixed, and colors swirled around them like pinwheels. Somehow I remember the only attire that all of the Pygmies had in common was the Nike running shoes they wore in spirited races up and down the beach.

When the Pygmies left Cumberland, their tracks were still on the shore. GoGo went back and videotaped the tiny footprints they left behind on the beach. I'm still glad she did. For once the tide had come in and the winds quickened, they completely erased the last remnant of their visit. Without her videotape, no one might ever remember that the Pygmies had been here. ✒

Lucy Ferguson's Dying Day

One particular day in summer, I awoke and was no more. It was as simple as that. I knew the turkeys needed tending, the cows a last shove and some hay. I had a final glimpse of my grandson going about his day's tasks at the old Inn. It was sunny. The sand was hot underfoot, but I knew this mostly from habit for by 10:30 a.m. I was already starting to lose feeling in my feet and legs. They knew the path to Greyfield well, though, and we drove down the Main Road one last time.

At home the nurses bothered me with efforts to eat. I was not in need of any nourishment they could provide. I waved them away from the bed, tired of the attention. Ready to go.

One or two phone calls on the two-way radio. The disembodied voice of someone I've known all of my life rattles on about I care not what. Good-bye. That's all I want to say. Good-bye. I'm not leaving, really; not really going anywhere. I feel more like I'm just going in. As if the day is done and all my energy is spent. One decent night's sleep. Please. And some silence. Silence from human voices anyway. Give me more of the kind of silence I found on the beach. Crashing surf, gulls above screaming, laughing at my naked old body sleeping in the sand while a jeep makes tracks around my solitude. The non-silence of the woodpeckers and ospreys swooping, remembering, searching, haunting this Island I know as home. That kind of silence. All these years they thought I was deaf.

And emptiness. I crave the emptiness of myself. The black water of a tidal pool reflecting my nothingness. I relish the prospect of never needing to be filled again. Just walking. My shadow and the shadow of the alligator behind me looming long and black in the white hot sandy bank. This is what I will tell them of nothingness: the deep black pool of an alligator's eye.

Good-bye.

At the memorial service for Lucy Ferguson several months later, we were joined by a stallion that kept his distance but made his presence known by boldly snorting and dancing in the sand nearby. Even those who do not believe in the reincarnation of the spirit wondered, long and hard, if that stallion could possibly be Lucy.

FOOTNOTE: *Several years later, I was invited to speak before a Methodist Sunday School class in Atlanta, Georgia, regarding my spiritual experiences living on a natural island. The idea was to see how it could help us in our everyday life. After pondering a possible subject matter for quite some time, the date of Lucy's death came to me. Why would the death of a human being help me in living a spiritual existence during this lifetime?*

I related how Lucy's nurses told me that she awoke on that particular morning knowing that she would die that day. How she got them to drive her to Greyfield one last time to see her relatives and employees, to help her hobble on her walker among her raised wild turkeys, diverse colored pheasants, and all of the other animals at her home. She was able to have a connection with animals that only a deaf person will ever understand.

I then told to those listening to this tale and searching for a way of living their own lives, how Lucy laid on her bed at approximately 11 o'clock in the morning with her feet already cold. And how as the next two or three hours passed, her legs began to get colder and colder, with no movement. Then her hands and arms, and all the while she was holding the hand of her beloved nurse. And then she was gone. The perfect scene.

For years I have pondered that scene. I explained to this church group that Lucy Carnegie Ricketson Ferguson was able to experience that particular death ritual because she approached her life with a similar ritual. If I live my life to the fullest, I have a much better opportunity of leaving this life in a way that is beautiful, emotionally healthy, and spiritually rewarding. Lucy Ferguson did not wait until her death to find heaven — she was committed to being there every day of her life.

Give me more of the kind of

silence I found on the beach.

Listen to the voices.

—Linnaeus

THORNTON W. MORRIS
Author

Thornton W. Morris is a resident of Cumberland Island, Georgia. He graduated from the University of Georgia School of Law and serves as the managing member of Morris Law Firm *(a Limited Liability Company)*, Atlanta, Georgia.

Thornton is also President of Cumberland Legacy, LLC, a multiple-family office, and has developed a unique and innovative approach to helping families with some of the issues that face individuals possessing inherited wealth. As part of his consulting in this area, Thornton speaks frequently with various families regarding the challenges inherent in the generational transfer of wealth.

One of Thornton's proudest accomplishments has been the authoring of the Cumberland Island National Seashore legislation and the shepherding of it through the Congressional process, resulting in its signature by President Nixon. Since that time, Thornton has been active in representing the owners of Cumberland Island, and of other natural areas, in the transferring of properties from private to public use. In these efforts, Thornton has sought to find a reasonable balance between the preservation of America's natural resources and a long-range strategy for the efficient use of our Country's pristine areas. He is the President and founding Director of The Cumberland Island Conservancy, Inc.

Thornton Morris has spent his adult career in balancing his life's work between business, family and personal relationships, and the protection of our country's pristine areas. He is a frequent speaker to members of the legal and accounting professions, as well as financial, business, and leadership groups. He has been interviewed or quoted by such organizations as *The Wall Street Journal*, CNN, BBC, BBC World, NPR, ABC, CBS, and NBC, and by the various regional and national wire services.

DAVID HAYNES
Photographer

A professional photographer since 1975, David Haynes' work has included photojournalism, portrait and wedding photography, and commercial and advertising photography. He now focuses on fine art photography, portraiture, and teaching photographic technique. He also writes a monthly magazine column for *Alabama Living* Magazine.

As a newspaper photographer and editor, Haynes was recipient of more than 40 newspaper photography awards from 1982-89. Since leaving the newspaper business, Haynes' images have been in numerous publications in both editorial and advertising and have been featured in a number of gallery exhibitions. At the turn of the 21st Century he used an 8x10 view camera and black-and-white film for a year-long project that documented life in Alabama during the Year 2000.

The following year Haynes was awarded an artist fellowship grant by the Alabama State Council on the Arts for 2001-2002, recognizing his work as a significant artist in Alabama.

Haynes now lives and works in a home studio in The Village at Blount Springs, a planned community 30 miles north of Birmingham, Alabama. His business – The Studio at Blount Springs – features portraiture, fine art prints, and photographic workshops and outings.

For more on Haynes' work visit his website at:
www.studioblountsprings.com

DON HARBOR
Photographer

Don Harbor has been in the advertising and design business since 1966. As an art director his passion was always photography. Over the following thirty years he commissioned work with many great photographers and cinematographers, carefully watched and listened to them as they worked and played, learned many valuable lessons, and had a lot of fun. In 1996 he retired from art direction and became a full time photographer. He works primarily in black and white using a variety of cameras of various vintages in formats from 35mm to 8" x 10". Don does all of his own darkroom work, which gives him total control from start to finish. His work as an art director and as a photographer has frequently appeared in many design awards books including *Communication Arts*, the New York Art Directors Club, The One Show, and the *British D&AD Annual*.

DON M. BAGWELL & TERRY HULSEY
Digital Impact Design, Inc.

Founder of Digital Impact Design, Don is creative director with more than 26 years of conceptual design, sales and marketing experience in graphic design & creative communication. He is a 1974 UGA graphic design grad who has won numerous national and regional design awards in both print and digital media. His associate Terry Hulsey's skillset is a result of some 20 years designing for print and web, with an eye for high-impact, standout graphics.

ACKNOWLEDGEMENTS

I feel amazingly fortunate to live on Cumberland Island, Georgia. I have a beautiful marsh at my front, with a creek running beside my house, and all behind me is the forest. All of this has given me a richer life and has inspired this book. And from Cumberland came the characters that are described in this book.

A majority of the beautiful images are from the photographic genius of Don Harbor of Birmingham, Alabama, and David Haynes of Blount Springs, Alabama. They spent endless hours acquiring the images. Gratitude also needs to go to my friend Barbara McDowell, originally of Pittsburgh, Pennsylvania, and most recently from Providence, Rhode Island, for the photographs of her grandmother, Lucy Ferguson. Also thanks to Janet "GoGo" Ferguson for other photographs of Lucy Ferguson, and to Jim Boyd of Boyd Printing, for his images.

Also, the appreciation of my home and its value to me is only increased by the quarters of my son, Thornton Jr., and his wife, Ann, and their two daughters, Rachel and Emily; my son, Scott; and my daughter, Vann, and her husband, Paul. The knowledge that MorrisTown will also be a home to them gives me comfort.

I want to thank the late Coleman Carnegie Perkins for making MorrisTown available to me, and his children who are my nearest neighbors. A special thanks goes to Kate Perkins Hartsfield for the photograph of Coleman which appears in this book.

This book would never have been possible without the tireless effort of my friend, Don Bagwell of Cornelia, Georgia. Without Don's consistent support in helping me get to the essence of each of the vignettes and peeling back the language to get to my own feelings, the writings would be quite different. And without his peerless ability to match images with words, the book would not have been, in my opinion, nearly as interesting. Thank you, Don.

And finally, I want to thank Patricia Beman for reviewing the manuscript and getting some of the more obvious redundancies out of it.

— THORNTON W. MORRIS

A Few of the Recently Written Books Regarding Cumberland Island

Cumberland Island: A History by Mary R. Bullard (2002)

Robert Stafford of Cumberland Island: Growth of a Planter by Mary R. Bullard (1995)

Cumberland Island National Seashore: A History of Conservation Conflict by Lary M. Dilsaver (2004)

Cumberland Island, A Treasure of Memories by Larry F. Andrews, H. Grant Rice, and Joanne C. Werwie (1986)

The Seasons of Cumberland Island by Fred Whitehead et. al. (2004)

Cumberland Island: Strong Women, Wild Horses by Charles Seabrook (2004)

Cumberland Island (Images of America) by Patricia Barefoot (2004)

A Cumberland Island Adventure by Elizabeth Geiger Wilkes (2006)

Palindrome by Stuart Woods (1991)